MW00395765

WHO KILLED
JACKIE BATES?

For Jackie and Harry,

who should have grown old together

WHO KILLED
JACKIE BATES?

BILL WAISER

FIFTH
HOUSE

Cover and interior design by Dean Pickup
Edited by Lesley Reynolds
Proofread by Liesbeth Leatherbarrow

The type in this book is set in Centaur.

The publisher gratefully acknowledges the support of The Canada Council for the Arts and the
Department of Canadian Heritage.
We acknowledge the financial support of the Government of Canada through the Book Publishing
Industry Development Program (BPIDP) for our publishing activities.

 Canada Council **Conseil des Arts**
for the Arts **du Canada**

Printed in Canada at Friesens on 100% PCW ,
Forest Stewardship Council (FSC) Approved paper

2008 / 1

First published in the United States in 2009 by
Fitzhenry & Whiteside
311 Washington Street
Brighton, Massachusetts, 02135

Library and Archives Canada Cataloguing in Publication

    Who killed Jackie Bates? / Bill Waiser.

Includes bibliographical references.
ISBN 978-1-897252-18-5

    1. Bates, Jackie. 2. Bates, Ted. 3. Bates, Rose. 4. Filicide—
Saskatchewan—Eagle Hills. 5. Murder—Saskatchewan—Eagle
Hills. 6. Saskatchewan—Social conditions—20th century.
I. Waiser, W. A. II. Title.

HV6535.C33E23 2008   364.152'30971242   C2008-903438-4

Fifth House Ltd.
A Fitzhenry & Whiteside Company
1511, 1800-4 St. SW
Calgary, Alberta T2S 2S5

1-800-387-9776
www.fitzhenry.ca

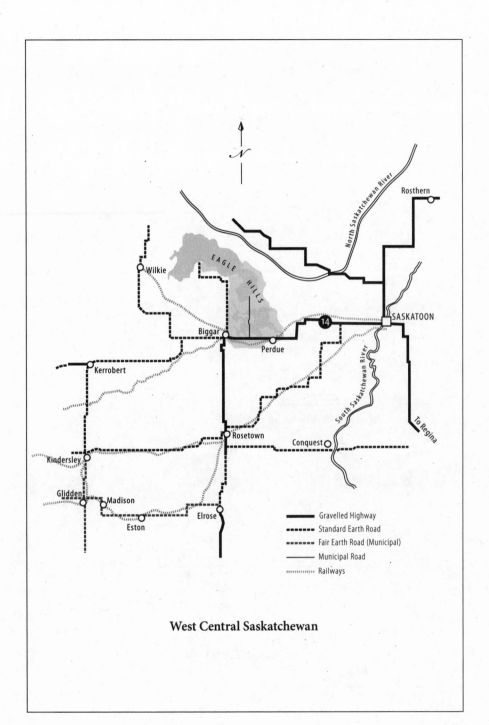

West Central Saskatchewan

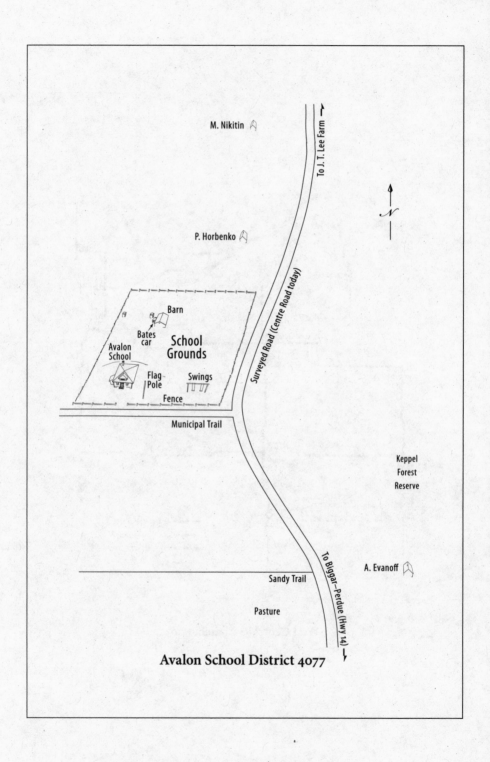

M. Nikitin

P. Horbenko

To J. T. Lee Farm

Surveyed Road (Centre Road today)

Barn

Bates car

School Grounds

Avalon School

Flag Pole

Swings

Fence

Municipal Trail

Keppel Forest Reserve

A. Evanoff

Sandy Trail

To Biggar–Perdue (Hwy 14)

Pasture

N

Avalon School District 4077

CONTENTS

WE HAVE BEEN MIXING THINGS UP

It was one of those life-altering moments. The irony is that he was there only by chance. In the late morning of Tuesday, 5 December 1933, Constable Donald McLay of the Rosetown Royal Canadian Mounted Police detachment was dispatched to the Eagle Hills to check into a car that had been parked overnight in the Avalon schoolyard. This seemingly routine matter would normally have been handled by Corporal Charles Carey of the Biggar office, since the hills, just to the east, were part of his district. But he was away for the day attending to another case.

McLay's superior, Patrol Sergeant H. W. H. Williams, was also busy investigating an overnight break-in at a Rosetown warehouse. It consequently fell to McLay, with just three years' service in the police force, to respond to the call and, in the words of Williams, "take whatever action the facts might warrant."[1]

What McLay found at Avalon was a grey Chevrolet coach, bearing Saskatchewan plates, on the west side of the school barn. It seemed as if the driver had deliberately parked the vehicle so that it was hidden from the road. McLay briefly inspected the car exterior and tried to look inside, but all the windows were frosted over. He then opened the driver's door and discovered three people—a man, woman, and child—in the back seat, covered in an old cowhide robe with their feet resting over the turned-down front seats.

The man, sitting wide-eyed in the left rear, had his arms upturned in front of him, seemingly in shock from his handiwork. Both wrists had been cut, one in two places. The woman, in the right rear, was bent forward with her head down as if she were silently praying, with a blood-soaked towel pressed tightly against her neck. There were other bloody towels in front of her on the robe. In the middle was a young boy, completely prone except for his head, which was awkwardly propped up against the back seat. He could have been asleep, but his yellow face and blue lips suggested otherwise.

Constable McLay was not the first person to set his eyes on the macabre scene. That dubious distinction belonged to farmer Pete Horbenko and his wife, Nellie. The couple, huddled together on the seat of an open democrat wagon, was on their way to Biggar around nine that morning. Horbenko was one of several men who had seen the mystery car the night before, and as he passed the school grounds the following morning he stopped to see whether the vehicle was still parked behind the barn. It was.

Horbenko wanted a closer look even though his wife tried to hold him back. He climbed down from the high wagon seat, walked over to the car, and knocked tentatively on the driver's door. No answer. He knocked again, this time harder, and called out, "Is somebody in there?"

A voice from inside said, "Yes."[2]

Horbenko cautiously opened the door and was immediately struck by the faint smell of gas. Peering inside, he saw a man and a woman in the back seat, with a boy, lying motionless, between them. In broken English, Horbenko asked the man why they had parked overnight in the schoolyard when they could have got help from one of the local farmers. The man replied that they had had car trouble. Horbenko then asked about the bloody scratches he saw on the man's arms. The man said that he had hurt himself trying to crank the car.

Horbenko also wanted to know about the woman, who was leaning forward in the back seat with her face deliberately turned away from him. He could see that she was bleeding from the left side of her neck and asked whether they needed a doctor. The man reported that they had been sick, but that they would be alright.

After a few seconds' hesitation, Horbenko closed the car door and went to retrieve his wife, who was waiting nervously in the democrat. He asked her to speak to the woman, to try to find out what the trouble was. But Nellie Horbenko didn't have any more luck than her husband in getting answers as to what the three strangers were doing there. The woman refused to acknowledge them in any way, as if she were deaf to their questioning, while the man kept insisting that they would be fine and didn't need to see a doctor.

It was obvious, though, that something terrible had happened during the night. Looking furtively around the car, the farm couple noticed two knives, one large, the other small, near the man's knees and some bloody towels next to the woman. But it was the fate of the young boy that concerned them most. "I thought he looked dead," Mrs. Horbenko later recalled.3

Unsure of what they were dealing with, the Horbenkos gently encouraged the man to get his family out of the cold and into one of the farmhouses nearby. He promised he would. They then closed the car door and hurried over to the Evanoff home, just across the road, with news of their grisly discovery.

Archie Evanoff, who had first seen the car the night before, immediately told his son Nick to ride the four miles to the Pooler farm, the closest place with a telephone, and call the RCMP detachment in Biggar. He also sent one of Nick's chums, Chris Dafoe, to fetch Jack Lee, an English settler and one of the school trustees. Maybe he could talk some sense into the couple in the car, especially since the Horbenkos said the man spoke with an English accent.

Lee had just finished his morning chores when an excited Dafoe arrived on horseback, motioning wildly about a car in the schoolyard and people with guns and knives. At first, Lee thought the young man had gone mad, but he eventually set off just before lunch for the Evanoff farm to find out for himself what was going on. After speaking with Archie, Pete Horbenko, and their neighbour Mark Nikitin, Lee realized that they were talking about the same people who had had supper at his place the night before. But before he had time to check out the car and confirm that it was the same family, Constable McLay arrived from Rosetown.

The young Mountie did not reach the school until just past 1 P.M. Little did he realize at the time that the injured man and woman, along with their dead child, had been in their makeshift tomb for about sixteen hours. After opening the car door and making a quick mental note of what he saw, McLay identified himself as a mounted policeman and asked the couple for their names. He was told they were Edward and Rose Bates. McLay then asked what had happened.

Rose spoke first, saying that her son, Jackie, had died from the car fumes and that in her grief she had told her husband to cut her throat. "I told him to do it," she declared. "Honest I did."4

McLay wanted to know if this was true. Ted said yes, that he had used his penknife. The constable had other questions for the couple, but decided that his first priority should be to get them out of the cold and to the nearest hospital before the woman's condition grew worse. Judging by the towels, she had lost a lot of blood. He helped Rose squeeze out of the door on the passenger side, next to the barn, and then slowly walked her over to his patrol car. Ted, with the front of his coat covered in dried vomit, was able to get out of the back seat on the driver's side and walk on his own.

McLay then checked to see whether Jackie was indeed dead, but made sure not disturb the position of the boy's body in any way. He also took a quick look at the gauge for the gas tank and noted that it read "empty." To ensure that no one tampered with the car and its contents, McLay called over Nick Evanoff, who was watching from the school gate along with several other local kids, and told him to stand guard. He then drove the Bates to the Evanoff home so they could warm themselves before he took them into Biggar. He never thought to ask whether the couple wanted to say goodbye to their son as they left the schoolyard. Nor, for that matter, did they make any such request.

At the farmhouse, McLay helped Rose out of his car and sat her in a chair beside the fire. She was still clutching a bloody towel to her neck. Jack Lee, who had been waiting with some of the local men, took Ted by his arm when he reached the door and led him to another chair. Lee had already guessed that it was the Bates' car behind the school, but he didn't expect to see the couple in such rough shape.

Putting his hand on Ted's shoulder, he said, "My God, man, what happened?"

Ted, chilled and shaking, lamely replied, "We have been mixing things up."

Lee persisted, "Why didn't you tell me this last night?"[5]

Ted answered that he didn't want to tell him his troubles, didn't want anybody to know their troubles. But there was no hiding from the truth that day, no denying that a young child had died under peculiar circumstances in an isolated rural schoolyard.

Constable McLay set off for Biggar, about fifteen miles away, once the couple had warmed up. He asked Archie Evanoff to ride along with Ted in the back seat of the patrol car in the event he needed assistance. During the trip, the policeman asked Mrs. Bates about her wound, wanting to make sure he had understood her correctly when she claimed at the school that her husband had cut her throat. She repeated what she had told him earlier, adding that she thought the penknife was in her husband's pocket. McLay then asked Ted whether he had the knife. Ted said yes, took it out before an incredulous Evanoff, and calmly handed it to the Mountie as he drove west along Highway 14.

The young constable had other questions about what had happened in the parked car during the night, but they would have to wait until Biggar. His only concern at the moment was getting the couple to a doctor as quickly as possible. He didn't want two dead bodies on his hands.

CHAPTER ONE

EVERYONE
LIKED HIM

It's not known when Ted Bates first arrived in Canada. It could have been 1912 or maybe even two years earlier. His name is found twice in the Canadian census for 1911, as a single boarder in Toronto and Winnipeg, but the date of birth is wrong in both instances. His life was like that—in many respects, a mystery. He seemed to want it that way.

What is certain is that the twenty-three-year-old Bates was aboard the S.S. *Victorian* when it docked at Saint John, New Brunswick, on 10 April 1914. He was sailing from Liverpool, England, on ticket number 3800. He was one of 506 passengers in steerage, the cheapest rate below deck in the bowels of the ship. According to the information provided on the steamship's manifest, Ted had been farming for four years, two of them in Ontario, perhaps in Woodstock. That's where he was reportedly headed upon his return, this time to stay.

Bates might have been travelling with an English buddy, twenty-five-year-old Joseph Childs, who provided strikingly identical information about what he had worked at and where he was going. In fact, it is quite likely that the pair first immigrated together, childhood friends on an overseas adventure. Now they were classified as "returning Canadians" by immigration authorities.[1] Bates' stated occupation is also something of a puzzle. He had never been near a farm, let alone worked on one, before coming to Canada. He was actually from one of the poorest areas of London.

Edward Alfred, known as Ted, was born in Blackfriars Road on 7 December 1890, and lived at 27 Gray Street. Blue-eyed with dark brown hair, he was the only son of a printer's warehouseman, Edward Bates, and Alice Ewin, and was named after his father and his father's younger brother, Alfred, a coal porter. By 1901, Edward Bates senior was dead, and young Ted, his widowed mother, and two sisters were living with his aunt (his mother's sister) and uncle, a childless couple, down in Byfleet, about twenty miles southwest of London.[2]

Life would have been difficult, if not penurious, for the fatherless Bates family, but Ted somehow managed to complete his schooling, at least that's what he claimed much later in life. What he did in his mid-teens is another matter. It's quite probable that this is when he trained for his future trade as a butcher. It also appears that he chafed at helping support his mother and younger sisters and wanted to get out from under his dead-end life in England. Canada offered him the chance to strike out on his own, to make something of himself and his future.

When Ted Bates headed for Canada, he joined the hundreds of thousands of British immigrants who made the dominion their new home in the new century. At the time, Canada was the land of opportunity. After several disappointing decades of sluggish growth, the Canadian economy went into overdrive in the late 1890s, sparked by an unprecedented world demand for Canadian commodities, lower shipping costs, and the discovery of gold in the Klondike and South Africa.

The boom seemed to signal that the country's great promise was finally to be realized. The prime minister, Sir Wilfrid Laurier, certainly believed so. He declared that the twentieth century would be Canada's century as assuredly as the nineteenth had belonged to the United States. Census data substantiated Laurier's claim. In 1901, for the first time in three decades, more people came to Canada than left. What enticed many of these immigrants to Canada was the prospect of own-ing 160 acres of free land. In the early 1890s, the United States had exhausted its homestead land, prompting historian Frederick Jackson Turner to declare the end of an era in American history. Almost overnight, the Canadian prairies were transformed into "the last best West." An advertiser could not have asked for a more appealing image.

The federal Department of the Interior circulated millions of promotional brochures, sponsored displays at exhibitions, financed western tours for journalists, and struck secret deals with steamship agents to direct prospective settlers to Canada. One popular guide even boasted that "all that is needed is a mere scratching of the soil" to bring the virgin prairie under cultivation.[3] These promotional efforts paid handsome dividends. More settlers applied for homesteads in western Canada in the first decade of the twentieth century than dur-ing the entire previous century.

Bates, however, was not really the kind of immigrant that Canada wanted. The Department of the Interior was more interested in settlers with practical farming experience, who would stay on the land and turn the prairie wilderness into productive farms. But even though people of peasant stock were recruited in record numbers from central Europe, the British topped all other immigrant groups during this period. They were still preferred over other nationalities, as evidenced by the fact that the federal government spent more money advertising western Canada in Great Britain than anywhere else.

A lack of agricultural experience did not stand in the way of prospective British settlers like Bates. The chance to secure 160 acres tended to attract people with little or no farming background in the naive belief that bringing the land under cultivation would be relative-ly easy. Indeed, there was no shortage of pandemonium at Dominion Lands offices when new areas were opened to homesteading. Who wouldn't want to stake their claim to a new beginning, especially when it cost only a ten-dollar entry fee for a quarter-section of land?

According to federal land records, Ted never applied for a western homestead. Instead, he evidently decided to work as a hired hand in Ontario, gaining valuable farming experience and much-needed capital before venturing westward. It was a smart decision. To secure title, or what was called the "patent" to their quarter-section, homesteaders had to meet certain basic requirements by the end of three years: they had to live on the land for six months each year, erect a shelter, and cultivate at least fifteen acres. These duties might not seem too onerous, but many a settler was defeated by them. Between 1871 and 1930, two out of every five homestead applications in the three prairie provinces were cancelled. The failure rate actually climbed above 50 per cent during the last two decades of the program. Perhaps fellow Englishman W. C. Pollard put it best when he suggested that homesteading was "a gamble in which the entrant bet ten bucks with the Government against 160 acres of land that he can stay on it ... for three years *without starving*."[4] Those with little capital, and even less farming experience, had a greater chance of starving.

Bates, for his part, apparently started to doubt what he was doing—unless it was nothing more than a lark to begin with—and headed back to London in the fall of 1913. It was highly unusual for immigrants to return home again, especially for those with few resources to fall back on. Most never did. It was as if they had closed a door on their former life. Ted might have been homesick and simply have wanted to see his family and friends. Or had he gone overseas just to check things out? His visit home, however, lasted only the winter and his return to Canada aboard the *Victorian* suggested that he was going to stay this time.

Where he would stay was another matter. Although Ted told Canadian immigration authorities that he intended to continue to work in Ontario, his 1954 obituary in the *Rosetown Eagle* places him in Manitoba in 1914, and then later in Saskatchewan, but a search of provincial directories from the period does not turn up his name.

That's not surprising given the number of men on the move at the time. Western Canada was predominantly a male frontier in the early twentieth century, all the more so since women, except in rare circumstances, were denied the right to take up homestead land. Many married men also came west alone to get settled on their land before sending for their wives and children.

To survive their first few difficult years on the land, homesteaders often turned to off-farm employment. There were also large pools of low-skilled male labourers, usually young and single, who drifted from place to place depending on the job and the season, doing everything from working on the railways or other major construction projects during the summer to harvesting the crop in the fall to logging in winter. And that's how Bates could have ended up in Manitoba. Every August the railways sponsored what were known as harvest excursions, bringing thousands of migrant workers from eastern and central Canada to the prairies at reduced rates. In 1908 alone, 27,500 harvesters made the trip west. Ted might have been among them in 1914. All carried within them the hope that they too might be able to get their own parcel of land one day.

Another big question mark hanging over Bates' activities during these years is how he avoided service in the Great War. Less than four months after he returned to Canada in 1914, the country marched off to war alongside Great Britain and the other dominions. The vast majority of the first recruits for the Canadian Expeditionary Force were recent British immigrants, reflecting the numbers that had poured into Canada over the previous decade. Sixty-three of the first sixty-eight volunteers from the Swift Current area, for example, were British-born. The story was the same at other recruiting stations across the prairie west.

Ted, though, did not sign up. Nor was he forced into service after the new Union government introduced conscription in 1917. There is no war record for him, a fact confirmed during the Second World War when he reported on his 1940 National Registration form that he had no previous military experience.[5] Why Bates refused to answer the call to arms is difficult to answer, especially given his nationality and age. The "how" is equally problematic. He might have been classified as medically unfit, but there is no surviving evidence of any health problems, unless one counts his weakness for booze and food. At five-foot-ten and 220 pounds, Ted was strong and stocky, an imposing figure, according to those who knew and remembered him.

Another possible explanation is that he was needed as a hired hand. The Canadian government had asked western farmers to grow as much wheat as possible for the Allied war effort. Producers responded by expanding their cropped acreage. At the same time, though, they had to contend with a severe farm labour shortage that saw harvest wages double. To help ease this problem, the government promised that there would be no conscription of young agricultural workers, including farmers' sons. But when the Germans launched a punishing offensive in the spring of 1918 that put the end of the war in doubt, Canada summarily cancelled all military exemptions. How Bates evaded being called up is anybody's guess.

In 1918, Bates was working on the Gatenby farm near Lemberg, Saskatchewan (between Regina and Yorkton). He left the following year for the west-central side of the province to start farming on rented land near Glidden, about thirty-five miles east of the Saskatchewan–Alberta boundary (the fourth meridian) and roughly halfway between Kindersley to the north (fifteen miles distant) and the South Saskatchewan River to the south.

Settlers had first moved into the region shortly after the turn of the century, following the Old Bone Trail running southwest from Saskatoon's 11th Avenue towards present-day Rosetown. The route across the open prairie was cluttered with sun-bleached buffalo bones that were collected for the fertilizer industry and shipped in boxcars from Saskatoon, hence the name of the trail.

In 1906, Allan Newcombe, who worked in Saskatoon's Land Titles Office and doubled as a land locator, brought a small group of American families from Boston to the area northeast of Glidden (north of present-day Madison). Those who stayed formed what was known locally as the Bostonia settlement and would reward Newcombe's efforts by naming the rural municipality (No. 260) after him.

The following year, two years after Saskatchewan became a province, George Gledhill, an accomplished musician by training, took out the first homestead west of Cutbank coulee near the site of the future village of Glidden. Gledhill's homestead application touched off a mini land rush. Nineteen homesteads were taken out in 1908, then another eighty-eight in 1909, seventy in 1910, and sixty in 1911. Among this last group of homesteaders was Ada Standen, an Ontario widow with six young children, who filed on land north of Glidden before opening a boarding house in Kindersley. She and her family, like many others, came to the district on the Canadian Northern Railway's new Goose Lake Line, which reached Rosetown in 1908 and then Kindersley the following year. The more hardy—or maybe fool-hardy—travelled to Swift Current on the Canadian Pacific and then trekked north by wagon or ox cart via the ferry at Saskatchewan Landing. A more direct route across the river was provided in 1914 by the Lemsford ferry, which was almost directly south of Glidden.

Incoming settlers could also buy land (sixteen of thirty-six sections) that the Canadian government had set aside in every local township for sale by the Canadian Northern to help cover its construction expenses. This included tens of thousands of acres controlled by land companies, such as the Madison Holding Company or the Ottawa Farm Development Company, which had purchased large swaths of railway land and then resold it. The J. E. Martin Land Company, for example, ran regular excursions from Minneapolis for prospective farmers.

There was no shortage of takers. Chase Glidden of DeKalb, Illinois, the nephew of the inventor of barbed wire, acquired eight sections (over five thousand acres) in the Bostonia district from the Martin Land Company in 1912. He was one of the few stampeders to make his fortune during the 1898 Klondike Gold Rush and decided to add to it by becoming Saskatchewan's newest wheat king. Glidden ran his farm operation with the same kind of raw optimism that fuelled the settlement boom. There was nothing modest about his expectations. While local homesteaders gamely struggled to bring a few acres under cultivation, he used two Rumley Oil Pull tractors, working in tandem, to break the prairie sod. The land in the area was generally level and varied from heavy clay around Glidden, to lighter loam to the northeast and west, and sandy soil near the river. It was a huge sweep of open prairie, originally considered part of the Palliser triangle.

In the late 1850s, a British scientific party, known as the Palliser Expedition, had assumed that the lack of trees was a sure sign of aridity and reported that the area south of present-day Saskatoon to the international boundary formed a triangle of infertile lands. Yet once Canada acquired the North-West in 1870, the southern grasslands were reassessed, but under completely different circumstances. Ottawa expected most, if not all, of its new western empire to be fertile. How else would it attract hundreds of thousands, possibly millions, of prospective farmers to the region?

Government surveyors and explorers consequently began to promote the benefits of homesteading the open prairies. Botanist John Macoun even claimed to have discovered a veritable agricultural Eden. But in truth, the agricultural potential of the open prairie varied from place to place and from year to year. Some seasons it could be a desert, others, a garden.

Glidden homesteaders had no difficulty producing decent crops their first few years on the land, but the more vexing problem was securing a rail line and ending the need for local farmers to haul their grain long distances to the nearest shipping point. It would also go a long way towards easing their sense of isolation. The Canadian Northern, anxious to generate local traffic, planned to build a new branch line west from Elrose to Alsask, paralleling its Goose Lake Line. By 1914, however, the track reached only as far as Eston, where construction was delayed because wooden trestles had to be built across the yawning Snipe Lake and Cutbank coulees. Then the war intervened, and crews finished clearing the grade as far west as Eatonia (the next town after Glidden) before work on the roadbed was suspended.

The timing could not have been worse. In 1914 a devastating drought caused a poor crop, but then the rains came at the perfect time the following summer, producing a mammoth harvest. Chase Glidden, who had continued to expand his land holdings, needed a remarkable forty days to get the crop off his fields, even with a sizeable work force sometimes working around the clock. One of his sections of land set the provincial yield record for 1915—an astounding fifty-seven bushels of wheat per acre. Some of the kernels were reportedly as large as peas. The harvest that fall literally plugged the grain-handling facilities in nearby Kindersley. It also confirmed the great agricultural hopes for the district. The Canadian Northern immediately resumed its construction program, setting aside a townsite at Holbeck, not far from the Gledhill homestead which operated a post office by the same name.

Holbeck enjoyed the distinction of lasting less than a year—an extremely short time, even for Saskatchewan where once-thriving villages can no longer be found today on the map. Donald Blair, who homesteaded in the district in 1911, built the first store in the new townsite in the spring of 1916. Other businesses quickly followed in anticipation of the arrival of the railway. What they got instead was heavy rain, and lots of it. Holbeck, sitting in a low-lying area, became a small lake. The water was so deep that Blair had to use a raft to take customers to his store, slowly picking his way through the floating lumber that was intended for a livery stable. The railway had no alternative but to relocate the townsite to higher ground, and soon, since steel was scheduled to arrive the next year.

The preferred site was about a mile east on land owned by Chase Glidden. The choice was doubly ironic. It was originally railway land and now the Canadian Northern wanted to buy back forty acres of it for the new townsite. It was also part of the same section of land that produced the record wheat yield in 1915. Glidden, understandably, was reluctant to sell, but eventually reached a deal. Maybe it was because the railway offered to name the village after him. Once again, Don Blair was the first merchant in the new townsite, after hauling his store from Holbeck to Glidden in 1917. And once again he was joined by other businesses in the certain knowledge that the railway would finally come through that October. There was no shortage of confidence about the community's future, even though the outcome of the war was still in doubt. If there ever was a classic prairie boom town, Glidden was it.

The transformation of Chase Glidden's prize wheat field into a clutch of commercial buildings with false wooden fronts was truly amazing. By the time the village was formally incorporated in March 1919, there were four grain elevators, two general stores, two lumber yards, two cafés, a hardware store, bank, drugstore, butcher shop, garage, poolroom and barbershop, real estate office, weekly newspaper, livery barn, Chinese laundry, municipal office, and school. Electricity was still another decade away, but there was a local telephone exchange that even offered service to rural subscribers by running the line along fences. The only major disappointment was the lack of potable water; even deep wells failed to find water that was safe to drink. The other problem was fire, which destroyed sections of the village with seeming impunity. One of the council's first purchases was a chemical firefighting unit.

What drew Ted Bates to the Glidden area in 1919 is not known and remains part of the mystery about the man. He could have heard about

10

the fine crops and decided that there was probably no better place to get into farming on his own, or he might have been advised to go there if he was just starting out. There's also the possibility that he knew someone there or read an ad in a newspaper about land for rent. In any event, he travelled more than halfway across the province, some 250 miles from Lemberg, to become a wheat farmer, maybe even a wheat king. He had watched for years as his employers had benefitted from the wartime appetite for wheat, and now it was his turn.

Bates could not have chosen a worse time to grow wheat for the Canadian export market. The end of the Great War was followed in 1920 by a stubborn recession that refused to let go for the next three years. As the shrinking economy tried to adjust to peacetime conditions, hundreds of businesses, including the Glidden branch of the Bank of Toronto, closed their doors. Commodities, the engine of the Canadian economy, were particularly hard hit. Wheat prices tumbled more than 75 per cent from a high of $2.63 per bushel in 1919 to a mere 65 cents in 1923. This collapse came as a cruel blow to farmers whose production costs and debt loads had steadily escalated during the war, and it effectively doomed small, marginal operations.

For the first time in provincial history, the number of farms actually declined in the early 1920s. The CPR, meanwhile, abandoned its plans to build near Glidden as part of a proposed branch line from McMorran to Empress. Less than a hundred miles of track were added to the province's rail network in the early 1920s.

Bates also had to contend with poor growing conditions for his crops. Winter came early in 1919, the year that Bates started farming, and the harvest, if it was still worth it, had to be delayed until the following spring. To keep the gophers from claiming a share of the crop, the Rural Municipality of Newcombe ordered five hundred packages of Kill-Em-Quick poison and another five hundred of Gets-Em-All. Drought came next, beginning in 1921 and lasting for three years. The records of the Rural Municipality tell a sorry tale about the almost yearly need to bail out local farmers with seed and fodder in the early 1920s. The municipality had to provide relief to forty farm families in April 1922.

Bates was not among them. He was not even in the country. With his great farming hopes humbled by recession and drought, he somehow scrounged together enough money to get home and sailed from Quebec City in early November 1921, a few weeks shy of his thirty-first birthday. Ted's return to England undoubtedly surprised his family. They had rarely heard from him in the seven years since his last visit. He was no longer part of their world. They also likely wondered whether he was home to stay, and if so, how he would fit into life in the new post-war Britain.

Ted's mother and two sisters, Helena and Emily, were now living together in a cottage in Addlestone, Surrey. His mother had married again, to a Mr. Hollock, but he was nowhere about. Ted's oldest sister and the one he seemed closest to, Helena, or Lena as she was called, had lost her husband during the war and worked as a domestic cook. She owned the cottage. His other sister, Emily, was married to a man named either Hartshorn or Scanes—both surnames were written in the back of the passport that Ted had recently been issued in Montreal. It is not known whether either woman had any children.

Bates spent the Christmas holidays with his family before looking for work. His search took him to Chichester on the south coast, about sixty miles from London. Here, he met Rose Slatter. The twenty-nine-year-old Rose was the daughter of Malachi and Esther Slatter, the fifth of seven children. Her father was the roadman for the district council in Rotherfield, Sussex. She had done light nursing during the war and was toiling as a cook when she met Ted.[6] Rose had limited education, but was fairly good looking—tall and slim, with shoulder-length black hair. It's a wonder she wasn't married, although it could have been because of her nervous disposition. Most people found her high-strung and difficult to get along with. Ted liked her though, and even told his family about meeting Rose in Chichester. But he was not ready to settle down. After what his older sister would later describe as his six-month English holiday, he boarded the *Empress of France* for Canada in early May 1922.

When Bates reached Quebec City later that same month, he was required to complete a separate entry declaration that the Department of Immigration and Colonization had just started using in 1921. On his form 30A, he indicated that he had previously entered Canada in 1914, but then crossed the year out and put down 1912 instead. No record for that date has yet been found. He also claimed that he had left Canada to visit his mother and that he was going "back to farm" in Glidden. Under "present occupation," though, he scrawled "nil."[7] It's more than likely that he did not know what he was going to do. Farming had been a bust, and it was certainly not a good time to go back to being a hired hand, given the depressed agricultural sector. That left only one real option—returning to the butcher trade, something he had probably done in London in his teens.

Glidden, however, already had a butcher. Maine-born Thaddeus J. Furse had first come to Kindersley in 1910 before setting up his own shop in the village in 1918. Bates consequently had to look elsewhere. He eventually ended up working in Conquest, a town about eighty miles to the east where the South Saskatchewan bent north and Canadian Pacific and Canadian National (formerly Canadian Northern) branch lines intersected one another. He knew the town because the CN train from Saskatoon to Glidden followed a circuitous route that included Conquest.[8]

Ted was there for about a year before another job opened up, ironically, back in Glidden. In fact, the two butchers did a switch; Furse went to Conquest, while Bates took over the Glidden business. The meat market was on the east side of the first block of Main Street, a road which ran perpendicular to the railway tracks and line of elevators to the south. It was a small building, only one storey high, with a large butcher's block and scale on the counter, hooks along one wall for hanging meat, and a cold room in the back. Behind the store was a small ice house with walls bulging with sawdust; the blocks of ice came from the South Saskatchewan River. It wasn't much, but for Ted it was a start, albeit a decade too late.

Bates readily fit into the community. He wasn't the only one in Glidden from a British background, or the only one who still spoke with a distinctive English accent. George V. Couper, who ran one of the two general stores, was proud of his "old country" heritage and acted as if the British were meant to run the world, if not rule it. His favourite expression was "Right-o." Postmaster and Great War veteran Tommy Grandage was English as well.

Most of the other businesses in the village were operated by people from Anglo-Canadian or Anglo-American backgrounds. In fact, whereas the local farm population included a number of immigrants from continental Europe, including Russian Mennonites, Glidden was a distinctly WASP stronghold. Couper's competitor, for example, was R. A. McDonald, a Nova Scotian who homesteaded near Dodsland before taking over Blair's general store. One of McDonald's best friends was drayman Stan Elliot, an anglophone from Quebec who originally ran the telephone exchange. Elliot's next-door neighbour on Railway Avenue was Imperial Oil agent and electronics expert Orville Galbraith, from Ontario. These same men dominated local government. Galbraith served three separate terms as village overseer, while Couper and Elliot held various positions on the village council up until 1960. Elliot was also the local justice of the peace and dispensed legal service from an office at the back of his livery barn.[9]

Bates' new business seemed to thrive, even though the Saskatchewan economy did not rebound from the recession until 1924. There was plenty of local demand for fresh meat, mainly because there was no electricity in Glidden and hence no refrigeration. Ted did some of his butchering behind the shop, but soon applied to the village council for permission to build a slaughterhouse on the nuisance grounds. He also secured an old sedan with a box built on the back for hauling meat. He was often seen travelling the grid roads in his quest to buy animals from local farms.

The butcher's friendly, affable manner quickly made him a popular figure in the community. "We all liked Ted," declared Mrs. C. H. Belton, the spouse of Glidden's blacksmith. Armand "Frenchy" Bisaillion, the butcher in nearby Eston, echoed her words: "He used to be real jolly, was a nice fellow and everyone liked him."[10] It was a common sentiment, shared by everybody in the village, except by one of its newest residents.

On 15 July 1924, after ten days at sea aboard the *Empress of France*, Rose Slatter stepped ashore at Quebec City with about thirty pounds in her possession. She reported on her immigration card that she was getting married and that she intended to be a housewife. If there were any doubt about her plans, Rose added that she—not her future husband—had paid for her own passage and that she would be catching the next train for Saskatchewan.

Coming to Canada at her own expense was a big step for Rose, but Ted had obviously regaled her with stories during their brief time together in Chichester during the winter of 1922. The pair had also kept in contact by letter, and once Ted got settled as a butcher in Glidden, they had talked about marriage. For the thirty-two-year-old Rose, still single, still struggling as a cook, there could have been no better future. Just like Ted more than a decade earlier, Rose had a chance to escape—the chance to leave one life behind and start a new one as a butcher's wife in small-town Saskatchewan.

Rose arrived in Saskatoon a few days later, getting off at the CN station that has since been replaced by a downtown shopping mall. Ted wasn't there. He was late. If that wasn't bad enough, the first thing he did was to ask Rose to loan him some money until they got to Glidden. On their way there, they stopped off in Conquest to see one of Ted's old buddies, a man by the name of Newby. He apparently convinced the couple to wed then and there, and within hours the ceremony was held in the Union Church manse by the local Methodist minister.

It may not have been exactly how Rose had imagined it happening, but her marriage to Ted that day was the first step in her new life in Canada. She had also made her first friend, the minister's wife, who kindly agreed to serve as her witness. Things were looking up after the bad start. The newlyweds headed next for Glidden, but when the train stopped at Eston, Ted left Rose there and continued on home alone. It was only later that the new bride learned that her husband was living with another woman at the time and had to deal with her before he showed up in the village with his new wife.

Ted returned to fetch Rose a few days later, having been on a drinking spree with her money in the meantime. He was "so drunk and silly," in her words, that "he did not know half he said or done." He drove her back to Glidden and "just dumped me off at another man's house."[11] Rose languished there for another two days before Ted found a place to rent for five dollars on First Avenue, one block north of Railway Avenue and around the corner from the meat market. The house, if it could be called that, was little more than a cottage, painted white with a sloping roof that leaked badly whenever it rained. Rose likened it to a henhouse. Ted rounded up some furniture, including a bed that had to be wired together, with a badly bowed, urine-stained mattress and musky pillows. There was nothing to cover the bare wooden floor. There wasn't even electricity or indoor plumbing, modern amenities that wouldn't reach much of rural Saskatchewan until the 1950s and 1960s.

What probably made things worse, if that was possible, was the place Rose found herself in. The open, treeless prairies of southwestern Saskatchewan were a foreign and discomfiting landscape, completely different from the world she once knew. So much for her dream home in Canada.

Her dream marriage was even worse. Ted, it turned out, was a heavy boozer. He was a regular client of Earl Forbes, the local boot-legger who lived across from the Bates' house and just a stone's throw from the meat market. Ted would either do his drinking there or in the back of his butcher shop, where he would often be found gambling. These habits gobbled up any money he made from the business. He didn't even have a change of clothes. Rose bit back her disappointment and asked her brother to send her the money she had left behind in England. She put thirty pounds into the house, the rest went into new clothes for her husband. Her gesture was greeted with Ted's confession that if she hadn't decided to come to Saskatchewan, he planned to get his widowed sister to tend house for him. At that point, Rose should probably have left, but now she had no money.

There was also another reason for Rose to stay. She was pregnant. On 12 October 1925, Rose gave birth to a boy, Edward Jack Bates, in Eston Union Hospital. Being a family man seemed to have a salutary effect on Ted's wayward behaviour, and according to Rose, things were okay for a while. Jackie's birth also coincided with the much-anticipat-ed return of prosperity.

Backed by higher wheat prices and ideal growing conditions, the province's farmers responded by sowing as much wheat as possible. The 1928 crop, at almost a third of a billion bushels of wheat, was the largest ever produced by any province or state in the world. The boom only encouraged producers to grow more wheat, some with the assis-tance of new power machinery. It also seemed to guarantee the future of places like Glidden, and the residents boldly invested in their com-munity during the latter half of the decade.

Some of the changes were quite modest, such as the replacement of the wooden sidewalks with cement ones, the installation of street signs, and the erection of a fire-bell tower. Others signalled the village's supreme confidence in its destiny, a destiny that included eclipsing its nearby rival, Madison, which had seven elevators to Glidden's four. In 1926, a large community hall was built, mostly with volunteer labour, on the north side of town. Two years later, a second storey was added to the brick school, doubling the number of classrooms to four. That was the same year that a small generating plant was purchased to provide power and light for the community. There was even talk within the village council in August 1929 of issuing a ten-thousand-dollar debenture for construction of a hospital.

These local improvements were accompanied by the establishment of a second newspaper, the *Glidden Star*, to rival the *Broadcaster*. A Ladies' Community Club was also organized, initially to raise funds to furnish the new hall, but it soon took on a wide range of charitable activities. Glidden, meanwhile, served as the hub for social activity, whether it was Sunday worship at the United Church, Saturday night movies in the community hall, or just getting the mail and supplies. Sporting events were also popular, bringing people together to play and watch, especially during the annual sports day, which showcased local talent. Three area farmers had tennis courts on their homesteads. There was also a golf course east of the village towards the Cutbank coulee. But the most popular sport was baseball, going back to the arrival of the first settlers before the Great War, and the Glidden Sodbusters were always competitive.

These were Glidden's golden years, and for a young boy like Jackie Bates, life was good. His best friend was Harry McDonald, who lived above his dad's general store across the street from the meat market. Although two years older, Harry, like Jackie, had no other siblings, and the pair were inseparable. They were forever running back and forth across the street between the two businesses, stopping long enough to play on the tractors at Bill O'Dowd's garage on the corner, or they'd holler and whoop it up along the gravel streets with Harry on his bicycle, Jackie on his trike. Every day through the summer, upon hearing the whistle of the approaching train, the friends would race down to the railway station and watch to see if any passengers got off or what freight was being unloaded. They would then head to the post office and hang around the entrance while the mail was sorted.

Sometimes they would drop in on Wes Robinson, the local tin-smith whose profanity was legendary, before slipping next door to watch blacksmith Bill Belton as he pounded red-hot iron fresh from his forge. The pair knew enough to stay clear of George Couper, who prided himself, at least in his own mind, on being the grand Pooh-Bah of the village. He was a menace to any young person. They adored, on the other hand, drayman Stan Elliot, who was raising a boy and three girls on his own after his wife had left him. Despite the hand he had been dealt, Elliot was a gentle, generous soul whose diminutive size masked his huge heart. Kids were always welcome at his livery business and fondly looked forward to St. Patrick's Day when he braided the manes and tails of his horses with green ribbons.[12]

Jackie attended the four-room, two-storey Glidden Consolidated School (No. 2726), one block north of his home. Because the school drew students from an almost seventy-square-mile area, it had a large population, even larger than Glidden itself (about 125 to 100). Horse-drawn vans, on wheels or skis depending on the weather, brought the country kids to the village each school day. The drivers would hunker down at the livery stable or poolroom, usually playing cards or getting caught up on the latest gossip, until it was time to run the rural students home.

Jackie stood out with his English accent. He was a little chubby and not very athletic, but he was bright. Neil Reimer, who came from a farm between Glidden and Madison and would later serve as the first leader of the Alberta New Democratic Party in the early 1960s, played "dibs" (marbles) and "cut the pie" with him in the schoolyard.[13] Jackie, though, was never allowed out in the evening. While the village kids played "run sheep run" or "hide and seek" under the new electric street lamps, he was kept inside. George Couper chalked it up to doting parents. Jackie, he once observed, "was the sunshine of their home ... they worshiped him."[14] Local children sensed it as well. Decades later, his former playmates use such terms as "prized," "sheltered," and "protected" when discussing Jackie's relationship with his mother and father. In fact, it's revealing to talk to these people today, who were pre-teens at the time, about the Bates family.

Ted, according to every informant, was a big, stout, jovial man, with a round florid face, huge hands, and a heavy accent—the epitome of a typical English butcher. No one knew about his drinking, but all recalled his friendly manner. Rose, by contrast, was a shadowy, reclusive presence. She was repeatedly described as aloof—a loner who rarely left the Bates home and never joined any of the local organizations or had much to do with other women in the village. She was also remembered as painfully thin, as if there were something eating away at her.[15]

What many Glidden kids did not know at the time is that Rose had probably reached out to the local women when she first arrived in the village. It was only natural to seek out female companionship after the rocky start to her marriage and then her pregnancy. There is an unidentified woman in the photographs of the women's community club in 1925 and 1926, and she bears a striking resemblance to the only known picture of Rose.[16] She also confided in a letter to Ted's sister Lena that she had sold some of her dresses to women she knew in Glidden to earn some pin money.

By 1928, Rose had managed to purchase the house on First Avenue with a twenty-five-dollar down payment. According to the old townsite register held today in an archival storage facility in Winnipeg, she paid two other instalments of the same amount over the next two years to secure the deed to the property. She also seems to have found the funds to cover the outstanding balance on the butcher shop. Her money management was quite remarkable given Ted's continued drinking and gambling. But as Stan Elliot once reported, "Mrs. Bates was the moving spirit in all their undertakings."[17]

Rose could only watch, however, as her marriage became a charade. Feeling lonely, if not abandoned, she increasingly withdrew from the world around her, while keeping a tight grip on Jackie, one of the few bright spots in her life. Many residents simply concluded that Rose did not want to fit in. Some even began to whisper that she believed she was too good for the village.

A few of the local men, though, apparently took pity on her for having to put up with Ted. Everard Joll, married with a family of his own, used to take Rose out for long drives; they were "pretty friendly," in his daughter's words.[18] Another man by the name of Wheeler (his first name was never given) regularly listened to her and her troubles. These acquaintances, and that's all they likely were, probably preserved Rose's sanity, but they alienated the women in Glidden, and in doing so, further isolated Rose.

While Ted, the easygoing butcher, went about town without a care, she sat for days inside their home, smoking the hours away as she dwelled on what had become of her and of the promise of a new beginning in Canada. She felt trapped in her marriage, trapped in Glidden, and probably in her darkest moments, trapped in her life. She stared at an empty future without much hope of anything. It wouldn't take much to push her over the brink.

CHAPTER TWO

JUST ABOUT OUT
OF MY MIND

arry McDonald, Jackie Bates' childhood friend in Glidden, will never forget the Great Depression. He was only seven years old when the world he knew was turned upside down. The experience seared an imprint on his memory that has not faded with time.[1]

He still vividly recalls, with his arms imitating the heavens, the huge towering dust storms that rolled over the prairies, leaving in their wake the smell and taste of dirt and an eerie brown haze that robbed the air of any moisture. He also remembers how his dad's once-thriving dry goods business limped along on relief vouchers. Even then, there were thousands of dollars in unpaid accounts that nearly drove the store into bankruptcy. Many of the debts would go uncollected, simply written off as an unavoidable legacy of the "Dirty Thirties."

Harry knows that he was lucky though. He never went hungry and always had a comfortable home in Glidden, while kids from the outlying farms came to school poorly clothed and poorly fed. No boy or girl, out of shame, wanted to talk about how bad things were, but the sadness in their eyes told of the hardship and deprivation that had taken over their young lives. McDonald's stories are part of the collective memory of the generation who lived through those "ten lost

WHO KILLED JACKIE BATES?

years." Surviving the Depression in Saskatchewan was like earning a badge for perseverance, and many older citizens like Harry wear it proudly today—and for good reason.

Much of Glidden's prosperity in the 1920s, like that of the rest of the province, had been fuelled by the sale of wheat on the export market. Now, on the eve of the new decade, agriculture was badly staggered by an economic and ecological one-two punch. International demand for wheat not only collapsed, but the price slumped to thirty-five cents per bushel by 1932—the lowest price in centuries!

The repercussions were catastrophic for Saskatchewan and its wheat kings. The average net income for the province's farmers went from $1,614 in 1928 to a mere $66 by 1933. With no money to run their operations, and already carrying outstanding loans for land and machinery, many could not stay on their feet. And when they went down, they took with them other sectors of the provincial economy: the retail, service, and transportation industries. Few were spared, if only because seven of every ten people, according to the 1931 census, depended on agriculture for their livelihood.

Saskatchewan would become the most heavily indebted province by the end of the 1930s, an almost complete reversal of the financial situation at the beginning of the decade. Perhaps two newspaper reporters said it best when they observed that life in Canada's wheat province had been reduced "to the lowest common denominator."[2]

The other nightmare was the prolonged drought that placed a stranglehold on the prairie region and would not let go for the better part of the decade. Severe dry spells had always been a persistent feature of the prairies, appearing on average every twenty years or so. The 1930s, however, were notorious for the number of consecutive dry years. Hot, drying winds scooped up loose topsoil and whipped it into black blizzards that made outside activity nearly impossible in places like Glidden. Darkness at noon was not uncommon, while churning soil piled up in deep drifts along buildings, fence lines, or ridges—anything that stood in the way of the swirling dust.

During the storms, mothers were known to put lamps by windows so that children could find their way home from school. They also faced a frustrating battle trying to keep the dust out of their homes, setting wet rags on window sills and hanging wet sheets over doorways. But the grit still managed to seep through, depositing a thick film on everything, like a layer of ash from a volcano.

"The sun through the dust looks big and red and close," Sinclair Ross wrote in his classic novel *As For Me and My House.* "Bigger, redder, closer every day. You begin to glance at it with a doomed feeling, that there's no escape."[3] Or as Edna Jacques put it less elegantly in "The Farmer's Wife in the Drought Area," one of her popular Depression poems: "The garden is a dreary blighted waste/The air is gritty to my taste."[4]

Since the country had experienced severe recessions before, as recently as the early 1920s, most expected the worst of the downturn to be over in a year, maybe two. There was no apparent need to abandon traditional practice for bold new initiatives, like spending money to get the economy moving again. No one at the time would have predicted that the nadir of the Depression in Saskatchewan would not be reached until 1937, when the drought extended its reach as far north as Prince Albert and the province's wheat kings produced the smallest wheat harvest in thirty years. By then, other parts of the country were already recuperating. It would take the Second World War to put Saskatchewan back on the road to recovery.

There was no such thing as unemployment insurance in the 1930s. Those in need of help were grudgingly given relief, or "the dole," as it was called at the time, typically seven dollars per family per month. It was deliberately kept as minimal as possible so that people would turn to it *only* as a last resort. Indeed, accepting relief carried the psychological stigma of failure and disgrace. The needy had to solemnly vouch that they had no other resources to fall back on—such as a bank account, personal belongings, or a relative—before they qualified for assistance. Government authorities and welfare experts justified this policy on the grounds that it was shoring up the moral underpinnings of Canadian society by preserving the work ethic. It seemed that the unemployed needed discipline more than they needed to be fed, clothed, and sheltered.

One of the other key relief assumptions was that men mattered more than women, resulting in what one commentator has called a "gendered" policy.[5] Men, especially those with families, were given priority, both in terms of relief assistance and relief work, because they were seen by society as breadwinners. There were no similar programs for women in Saskatchewan, even if they had once been part of the labour force and lost their jobs. The care of the unemployed female was understood to be a family duty, the responsibility of husbands, fathers, brothers, even uncles or male cousins, but certainly not of the state. In fact, in the early 1930s there was a backlash against women and girls in the workplace. They were collectively blamed for exacerbating the employment crisis, accused of being "bread snatchers and home wreckers."[6] Women, it was argued, should be forced to do the rightful thing and give up their jobs to men and go home where they belonged.

Many destitute people, overcome by shame, had to screw up their courage just to ask for help. One Saskatoon woman remembered seeing her father cry for the first time when he filled out his relief application for food for his hungry children. It was as if he was signing away his manhood. Another person was afraid that her reputation in her home community would be sullied if her request for help ever became public. "I don't know what to do. I hate to ask for help," confessed Mrs. P. E. Bottle of Craven, "Every one knows me around here and I'm well liked, so I beg of you not to mention my name. I've never asked anyone around here for help or cloths as I know them to well."[7]

Under the legislation creating Canada, the 1867 British North America Act, provinces and municipalities were solely responsible for the distribution of relief at the start of the Depression. Ottawa had no constitutional obligation to step in, and the federal government was not about to do so. Instead, it offered only temporary or emergency assistance up to a fixed limit. This rigid insistence on local responsibility put Saskatchewan communities on the front line in dealing with the crisis. Unfortunately, they were in no position to take up the battle. Most rural municipalities, including Newcombe, had been pushed to the wall by the collapse in agriculture and had trouble providing basic services, let alone dispensing relief. To make matters worse, ninety-five, or roughly one-third, of the province's rural municipalities suffered through their third consecutive year of crop failure in 1931. Saskatchewan's reputation as "next year country" seemed a cruel joke.

Premier J. T. M. Anderson initially put up a brave front about the deteriorating provincial situation but was reduced to vowing in a Yorkton speech in July 1931 that "no one in Saskatchewan would be allowed to starve."[8] One month later, he put his promise into action by establishing a new government agency, the Saskatchewan Relief Commission, to distribute direct relief (food, fuel, and clothing) and agricultural support (seed, feed, and fodder) to rural families. The rescue operation, costing 18.7 million dollars in its first year, was sorely needed. Nearly 50 per cent of Saskatchewan's rural population, or approximately three hundred thousand people, were assisted in one way or another. This aid was supplemented by the Red Cross which solicited donations of fruit, vegetables, and other foodstuffs from other provinces and then arranged for carloads to be shipped to distressed areas by the railways, free of charge. One of the bonuses was dried salt cod from the Maritimes.

Not unexpectedly, the weather, the misery, and the hopelessness spawned all kinds of exaggerated stories, many of which have become legendary. Children, it was said, reached school age before knowing what rain was or came running home in fright when they felt a drop of rain for the first time. Another story was that parents decided whether to send their children outside by throwing a gopher up in the air; if the animal dug a burrow, then there was too much dust swirling around. Or there was the young baseball player who lost his direction while rounding the bases during a dust storm and was later found several miles out on the prairie.

One of the best true-to-life sources is the gut-wrenching collection of letters found in the personal papers of Richard Bedford Bennett, Canada's Conservative prime minister during the first half of the 1930s. For many Canadians, his name was synonymous with the Depression. Some even mockingly suggested that R. B. stood for "rotten bastard." Dozens of people from Saskatchewan decided to write to Bennett in Ottawa about their troubles. Maybe it was because they had hit rock bottom and didn't know where or who else to turn to, or maybe they believed that Canada's millionaire prime minister might be moved to help them. Whatever the reason, the correspondence today serves as poignant testimony to what people in the province faced during these desperate times.

One of the most common problems was the lack of clothing. Mrs. Thomas Perkins of Kingdom turned to Prime Minister Bennett for help in ordering underwear from Eatons' catalogue for her elderly husband who was hauling wood and feed in the dead of winter. "I have patched and darned his old underwear for the last two years, but they are completely done now," she wrote in exasperation. "If you can't do this, I really don't know what to do. We have never asked anything of anybody before."9

J. A. Graydon of Regina, on the other hand, boldly asked for one of the prime minister's old suits: "Judging you by your picture I believe you are about the same size as myself ... I might say my people and I have always been staunch Conservatives. I wouldn't ask a Liberal if I had to go naked."10

The other major need was food. "I am five month pregnant," solemnly reported Mrs. C. L. Warden of Lambert, the mother of three, "and I haven't even felt life yet to my baby and it is I feel quite sure for the lack of food."[11]

Kids were not immune to the suffering. One of the most touching letters was prepared by young Dody Brandt of Harney, who wanted the prime minister to write a special letter for her and her little brother: "I just thought that I would write to you because I thought you would write Santa for me and tell him I was a good girl all the time, and Mama tells me her and Daddy have no money to give Santa for my little brother and me and we can't hang up our stockings now ... do you think Mr. Bennett he would forget Brucy and me ... I hope he don't."[12]

Any one of these letters could have been written by people from the Glidden area. It didn't really matter where you lived in rural Saskatchewan in the early 1930s. There seemed to be no refuge from the depressed prices and unrelenting drought that sent shockwaves through the provincial wheat economy.

At first, the village, in cooperation with the rural municipality, tried to devise make-work activities that would enable residents to pay off their tax arrears and overdrawn store accounts. Local farmers were hired to haul gravel for streets and roads or to clear the drifting soil that had been deposited, sometimes in dunes, by dust storms. Or they were called upon to sweep sidewalks, pull weeds, collect litter, shovel snow, and cut wood. But soon there were too many people in need and too few projects for them. A special meeting of the rural municipality in early April 1931 considered 111 applications for groceries, seed, feed, and fuel. Another 17 were received by council before month's end.

To put this demand into perspective, Newcombe had a population of 1,670 in 1931 (including Glidden at 123 and Madison at 101). Many of the applications were also likely from families. It is not too unreasonable to conclude that at least one-quarter of the people living in the municipality had come forward in need. There were undoubtedly others who refused to ask for a helping hand and never would. Several of the relief requests, according to surviving municipal records, had to be turned down for financial reasons. There was simply too much money owed in uncollected taxes on the books.

This sorry situation was helped somewhat by the creation of the Saskatchewan Relief Commission. Struggling residents could now apply to the provincial body for assistance by completing a one-page declaration about their personal situation. Since this kind of relief assistance was to be based on a recommendation from the rural municipality, local officials worked closely with their commission counterparts to come up with an accurate assessment of who needed help and what kind of help.

The estimate for Newcombe was seventy-five families requiring immediate aid and another two hundred families joining the list over the coming winter. But since the bulk of the commission records were destroyed in favour of keeping only a representative sample at the Saskatchewan Archives Board, it will never be known whether the rural municipality's recommendations were ever acted upon.

What is certain is that the rural population did not simply hunker down until the worst was over. There was no shortage of ideas of how to mitigate the impact of the Depression. Representatives from seventy-five rural municipalities meeting in Unity, for example, called on the federal government to get more involved in the provision of relief so that the burden did not fall so heavily on local bodies. Another gathering in Delisle suggested that rural municipalities be paid three dollars for every acre of crop failure. The College of Physicians and Surgeons of Saskatchewan even waded into the debate by arguing that medical services be included as part of the rural relief package.

These proposals, however, ran headlong against the deep-seated attitude that relief had to be dispensed sparingly or people might become hooked, as if it were some highly addictive drug that would sap recipients of their hope and initiative. President Walter Murray of the University of Saskatchewan voiced this concern as late as September 1933, when he put forward the idea of local farmers rounding up large field stones for future building projects on campus. "The danger of demoralization from idleness is increasing very rapidly," he warned the prime minister.[13]

What the sanctimonious Murray and other like-minded individuals didn't seem to appreciate was that people were not necessarily demoralized, but rather were profoundly disappointed by how their dreams for a better life had been snuffed out by the Depression. As Saskatchewan author Max Braithwaite explained in *Why Shoot the Teacher*, "They had come, filled with hope and vigour, to the 'Golden West' to make a new home" only to have "their souls scarred by a smouldering resentment and a keen sense of betrayal."[14]

That clearly was the case for those who had helped build Glidden into a thriving village in the 1920s. The once-vibrant community buckled under the weight of the Depression and would never really be the same again. Buildings, homes, and equipment fell into disrepair, while businesses that had existed since the founding of the village either collapsed or, in the case of Harry McDonald's dad's store, tried to stay afloat on the relief trade. Retail trade slumped so badly that the village council would eventually pass a bylaw requiring itinerant pedlars and hawkers to secure a special licence before selling any of their wares.

The rural municipality, meanwhile, severely reduced its activities since few residents were able to pay their taxes. It even toyed with closing the consolidated school in late 1932, in part because the village owed the school district nearly four hundred dollars for supplies and teachers' salaries.

Ted and Rose Bates, already treading water because of marital problems, were swept up in this tidal wave. Ted's butcher shop, like other village businesses, fell on hard times. Townspeople not only consumed less meat, but opted for poorer, less expensive cuts. Ted tried to make up the lost income by writing home to Lena in England and asking to borrow some money until things rebounded. All that his sister could afford to send him, however, was twenty-five pounds. Ted also continued to offer his butchering services to local farmers, readily taking a share of the meat in lieu of payment. But many of his customers found that they had been shortchanged in the end. Phyllis (Wilson) Nemrova, raised on a farm southeast of Glidden, remembers her father being among them.[15]

These questionable dealings never seemed to affect Ted's standing in the community. In April 1932, he was appointed one of five new village constables, complete with badges, ostensibly to deal with the transients who passed almost daily through the community on freight trains, looking for work. It was his job to see that their stay was as brief as possible by shooing them down the line to the next village or town. Ted also made an appearance before the village council to ask that a curfew for school-aged children be instituted. He evidently believed that kids should not be wandering the streets at night when there were so many strangers about.

Rose knew a completely different Ted, at least that's what she asserted in a disturbing, at times rambling, letter that she penned on Glidden Meat Market stationery to her sister-in-law Lena, probably in June 1932. Although her husband had straightened up after Jackie's birth, it was not long before he was back to his drinking and gambling ways. Rose reckoned that he had squandered from five to eight hundred dollars on booze during their eight years of marriage. She also maintained that Ted, not the Depression, was largely to blame for the meat market's financial woes. He avoided work at every opportunity and usually had to be retrieved from the clutches of the local bootlegger when someone wanted meat.

In the meantime, their relationship became increasingly strained. Ted rarely spoke to her, ignoring her for days, sometimes weeks, while Rose dismissed him as a lazy, callous boor, who didn't even have the decency to wash regularly. The pair had a secret, though. Ted had concocted a half-baked scheme to set fire to his shop so that he could claim the insurance and start over again—somewhere else.

Rose had another solution to their troubled existence. She would have preferred to have taken Jackie and washed her hands of both Glidden and her scoundrel husband, but Ted would not part with the boy, and Rose was not about to leave him behind. Feeling cornered, with no way out, she saw only one other option. "I am sorry to have to do what I am about to do but it can't be helped there is no way out," she began her letter to Lena. "He [Ted] has drove me to do what I intend to do," she continued in a spirit of resignation, "and I really can't go on any longer. I am just about out of my mind to know I have to stay for the boy's sake, but even the poor kid will be better off and so will I."

Rose then went on to describe how she regretted joining Ted in Canada and how married life with him had been a living hell. Nothing was left out. Telling Lena the awful truth about her brother Ted was like a form of therapy, a way of justifying what she had decided to do. "He is driving me mad," she declared at the end almost in defiance, "but don't let them think I am when I write this for I am never more sain in my life but I have just got to end my life and Jacks just because the man I got is an utter bad."[16]

The overwrought Rose never followed through on her plan. Who knows whether she ever intended to—whether she despised Ted enough to take her life and that of their son. She simply tucked the letter to Lena away as if it were unfinished business that she would return to one day. Her indecisiveness, though, when combined with her outpourings in the letter, suggest that she was close to a breakdown, and was maybe even manic depressive. It's actually quite amazing that she could still function with all the anger, confusion, and hurt that she was dragging around. But function she did.

Rose evidently convinced Ted that it would be best to get out of Glidden while they could still get something for the meat market. It clearly was a better idea than torching the building and then trying to submit a false claim for the insurance money. But they still had to find a buyer, no small feat when small businesses across the province had been hammered since the start of the Depression. A deal was eventually reached in the fall of 1932 with the Warmans, a large family that farmed northwest of Glidden. One might wonder why anyone would think that they could make a go of the meat market, but it was still early in the Depression and the Warmans probably believed, like many others at the time, that recovery was just around the corner.

Stan Elliot, wearing his hat as local justice of the peace, drew up the agreement of sale. He was also empowered to collect the outstanding balance on behalf of the Bates. What's not known, however, is exactly how much they got for the store, or whether Rose also tried to sell the house at the same time, or whether part of the proceeds was needed to cover any debts. A copy of the bill of sale, carrying Rose's signature as vendor, has never been located. Ted later stated that they had left Glidden with $1,400. He also claimed that there was more than $8,000 in unpaid accounts on the meat market books.[17]

The big question now facing the Bates family was where they were going to go. Thousands of other people on the move from the dried-out areas in the early 1930s opted to settle north of the North Saskatchewan River, along the southern edge of the boreal forest, where normal rainfall offered the prospect of growing a decent crop. Ted might have been tempted to head that way too, but Rose was not about to trade one Saskatchewan backwater for another. Her sole purpose in selling the butcher shop, according to Stan Elliot, was to flee to a large city. Elliot, who had been entrusted to wrap up their affairs in Glidden, was evidently the one person who knew that the Bates had decided to try their luck in Vancouver when they quietly slipped away in November 1932. Not even Harry McDonald got a chance to say goodbye to his friend Jackie. One day they were just gone.

Why Rose decided on Canada's third largest city is easy to understand. Vancouver, with about a quarter-million people, was a kind of mecca for the down-and-out, especially unemployed single men, because of the west coast's milder winters. It offered the Bates an escape from the dreary prairies and their seemingly dead-end lives in Glidden. They also likely believed that they had a better chance of getting back on their financial feet in Vancouver where there was greater opportunity, even if it was no longer in the butcher business. Most of all, it was probably closer to the world that Rose had imagined and hoped for in Canada—a large, modern city with a mostly British population. And she would not likely feel as trapped as she had been in Glidden, holed up in their little house like a nervous gopher.

Rose and Ted were terribly naive if they thought that they were getting away from the Depression on the Pacific coast. Vancouver, a major shipping port for bulk goods, had witnessed a dramatic decline in trade, made worse by the collapse in the demand for wood products, one of the mainstays of the provincial economy. Mill closures washed over the city's waterfront like mini tidal waves. A June 1931 survey, based largely on census data and relief registrations, found that almost half the male wage earners in all Vancouver industries had lost work time, if not their jobs. That was the same year that the overall unemployment rate for British Columbia topped 28 per cent, the highest for any province in Canada.

The situation would get only grimmer, thanks to the incoming flood of dust bowl refugees from the prairies. By 1932, the same year that the Bates family arrived, over two million dollars was being spent on relief in Vancouver alone. This amount would continue to climb over the next two years.

For western municipalities like Vancouver, desperately struggling to remain solvent as the Depression deepened, the simplest and most obvious way to keep their relief spending under control was to have Ottawa assume a greater share of the load. In particular, local officials argued that the tens of thousands of transients did not belong to any particular city or province and therefore should fall under national jurisdiction.

But as long as Prime Minister Bennett hid behind the Canadian constitution and continued to disclaim any direct federal responsibility for the unemployed, Vancouver had to find some other means to cull its relief lists or its services would be overwhelmed. The solution was the adoption and strict enforcement of a residency requirement. Only those who had lived in Vancouver for twelve successive months were eligible for assistance. This residency test proved an effective way to reduce the city's relief support, but there were those who pushed for other so-called reforms. It was proposed, for example, that Asians should not qualify for the same level of relief as the white population because they needed less to survive.[18]

That the Bates expected things to turn around for them in Vancouver suggests that, like many other Canadians, they saw the Depression as a short-term emergency rather than a long-term crisis. It would probably be over by the summer, if not the spring, of 1933. That was the popular sentiment as the country suffered through its third winter in the economic doldrums. Besides, for Rose, anywhere was better than Glidden, even if it took longer and cost more to get established. She even seemed willing to stick it out with Ted and try to make their marriage work. Her days in the village had been like a bad dream and Vancouver seemed light years away. She may even have wondered how the two places were part of the same country.

Drawing on the funds from the sale of the meat market, Ted tried his hand at the grocery business. He first operated the Cartier Grocery in Marpole, an established lower-middle-class/working-class neighbourhood on the southern edge of the city. He then ran another small store on East Fourth Avenue on the east side. It proved to be a bumpy ride. Ted had no practical knowledge of the Vancouver grocery trade, while his retail experience was limited to running the only butcher shop in a small town in rural Saskatchewan. He also chose a bad time to get started, especially when he had to feel his way in the dark.

Rose, for her part, might have hoped that a corner grocery store and its many demands would keep Ted occupied and out of trouble with the bottle. It was also the kind of small business that was relatively easy to get into, especially with real estate going so cheaply. The only catch in the plan was that competition in the tight market would be fierce. Real estate prices would also continue to slide to the point where property was nearly worthless by the mid-1930s, a complete reversal of the market today.

It wasn't long before both grocery ventures failed, but not before absorbing a good chunk of the Bates' money. But for some inexplicable reason, possibly at Rose's urging, Ted tried to break into the business a third time, taking over a grocery and confectionery store, The Triangle, at Fifteenth Avenue and Kingsway in June 1933. Maybe he believed that the two good luck charms—a British penny and Canadian nickel—that he kept above the bedroom door of their two-room apartment were bound to improve their fortunes. He would regularly look at them with Jackie and then turn to Rose and exclaim, "They'll change the tune for us, mother."[19]

That September, just weeks before his eighth birthday, Jackie started to attend Florence Nightingale School. He proved to have a quick mind and his teacher arranged to have him accelerated to the next grade later in the term.

In the meantime, his dad's new grocery business was going in the opposite direction, just like the first two stores. Feeling embattled, Ted wrote to Stan Elliot three times in the fall, imploring him to collect from the Warmans the $450 that was apparently still owed from the sale of the Glidden meat market. He even raised the threat of legal action, charging that the Warmans had not lived up to the sales contract and intimating that they could be put out of the store. But the money was never forthcoming, and understandably so. In the past year, the situation had gone from bad to worse in Saskatchewan and was not about to get any better in the foreseeable future. Nor had Ted learned anything from his latest business fiasco. If the Warmans had been able to pay even some of the outstanding balance—and Ted would have settled for that—he was seriously considering taking over yet another grocery store, this time "a good thing" on Fraser Avenue.[20]

By late October, Ted's lacklustre career as a Vancouver grocer had come to an ignominious end when he lost control of the Kingsway corner store. The last of the family's money was gone as well. Ted took to the streets to look for a job, along with hundreds of others in search of work, while desperately trying to find a buyer for the leftover grocery stock. He never let it be known that he and Rose were dead broke and was doggedly determined to keep it that way, even hiding the truth from their few Vancouver friends, the Gardiners and C. H. Babcock.

The teachers at Florence Nightingale were certainly fooled, especially when the Bates insisted on supplying Jackie's pencils and scribblers when they could have been obtained free at school. "He was always neatly dressed and seemed well fed," recounted Miss McIntosh, who had taken an instant liking to the little boy from his first day at school. Another teacher, Miss McKay, simply assumed that the family was reasonably well off. She had no inkling that the child's father had been forced out of the Kingsway store. And why would she? Jackie faithfully brought two apples to class every day and shared them with her at recess.

If anybody knew about the Bates' plight, it was their Kingsway landlord, Bob Wolstone. The first real sign of trouble was when Ted missed a rent payment. "He never said a word to me," Wolstone remarked, "but I could see what was happening." The landlord offered to carry the family for a few weeks, but Ted didn't want any charity, preferring to cover the overdue rent with some of their furniture. But it soon became painfully obvious that the family was in dire need of help, if only to put food on the table. Over Ted's feeble objections, Wolstone dropped off a few groceries, including meat. The former butcher, in turn, much like a condemned inmate on death row, began to open up to his landlord and told him the sad story of how the family had left

Glidden planning to start over again in Vancouver with the money from the sale of the meat market. "He always kept hoping that he would get paid what was owed him on the prairies," Wolstone recounted, "That was why he talked about buying a new store."[21]

The Bates stubbornly resisted applying for relief for as long as they could by pawning a few personal possessions. The sale of a ring and watch netted a princely six dollars. Finally, forced by necessity, a reluctant Ted put his pride in his pocket and walked into the city relief office in mid-November. He needn't have bothered. Even though he had valiantly tried to make a decent living for his family as a grocer, they were disqualified from assistance because they had lived in Vancouver for less than a year and could not meet the twelve-month residency requirement. Tragically, the Bates missed the cut-off by a matter of a few weeks.

Apologetic city officials directed Ted to the provincial relief office, where once again, hat in hand, he explained his personal situation and asked for assistance for his destitute family. British Columbian authorities, however, were just as keen as their Vancouver counterparts to keep a lid on the number of people they were supporting and advised him that he would have to take his family back to Saskatchewan. All they would do in the interim was give him a scrip order for five dollars' worth of food. This policy may have saved the province scarce relief dollars, but it effectively sentenced the penniless Bates family to a kind of relief limbo. If they wanted help, they had to return to Saskatchewan, but they had no prospect of getting there because they were stranded in Vancouver without any means of support. Here was a classic case of government bureaucracy at its worst.

Rose was floored by the news. The mere mention of the name Glidden conjured up all kinds of unpleasant memories that she had hoped to put behind her when the family relocated to Vancouver. The struggling village, on its heels because of the Depression, was the last place on earth where she wanted to live, and she bluntly told Ted so.

She had got out, while thousands of others were forced to stay in the God-forsaken, gritty Saskatchewan dust bowl, and she was not about to go back. There was no mistaking how she felt about it. Rose would never return to Glidden under any circumstances, even if it meant, she warned Ted, that she had to take her own life. It was a threat she repeated in the presence of her only close female friend, Ruby Gardiner, and her husband, Frank.

Ted shouldn't have been surprised by Rose's reaction. After all, he was largely to blame for their eight caustic years together in the village. Why would she knowingly want to relive them? The couple, however, had no other practical alternative if they were going to survive in Depression-stricken Canada. They were completely tapped out and could not count on any relief assistance from either the city or the province. It might have been different if they had had family or long-time friends to fall back on for help or maybe a loan. But even then, it meant swallowing their self-respect, something that Ted, in particular, could not stomach. No matter what way he looked at their predicament, he realized they had to return to Saskatchewan. And Rose would just have to go along, if only for the sake of their son and his welfare.

Getting Rose to see it that way, though, would be the challenge. Ted, for his part, was just as frustrated and upset by how their grand plans had gone so wrong in Vancouver. The past few days and weeks had been extremely stressful. It had been hard enough for him to apply for assistance—to declare to a complete stranger on the other side of a desk that he had failed as a provider for his family. But then there was the added indignity of being turned down, not once but twice, and told that his family had to return to Saskatchewan to get relief.

Ted, at the same time, rightly realized that he wasn't the one who should try to talk some sense into Rose; the pair's past history would only get in the way. So, he asked their friend Slim Babcock, who had been introduced to the Bates shortly after their arrival in Vancouver, to use his influence. As Babcock later recalled, a "very worried" Ted "asked me to speak to his wife in an endeavour to have her use her good judgement and take things in a proper way."[22]

Babcock didn't have much success. He innocently asked the couple one day when they planned to return to Saskatchewan. Rose immediately shot back that she didn't understand why they had to leave Vancouver. "After we've lost all our money, everything we have," she bitterly remarked, "we've got nowhere to go when we get back there."

Babcock probed a little deeper and found that Rose was distraught at the prospect that people in the village would learn that the family had been sent back to Saskatchewan because they were destitute. The shame of returning as a pauper and how it would set local tongues wagging was just too much for her to bear. "I can't go back Slim," she pleaded. "I would rather kill myself than go back to Glidden."[23] Babcock tried to tell Rose that she really didn't mean what she was saying, but she remained adamant. She would never set foot in Glidden ever again, and if forced to go, she would take her life.

Rose's intransigence left Ted scrambling to come up with another solution to their relief dilemma. After much soul-searching, they settled on a compromise. Since they couldn't stay in Vancouver and had to return to Saskatchewan, the couple decided to try to obtain relief in Saskatoon or some other place in the province. It still meant that they had to go back to the prairies, but it wasn't the same as having to go to Glidden. And that's what appears to have won Rose over in the end. That, and likely a promise from Ted that whatever happened after their return to Saskatchewan they would never go to Glidden. It's hard to imagine Rose agreeing to the compromise without that caveat. Ted probably had to swear to her that he would keep his word—and she would hold him to it. But just to make sure that they stuck to the plan, they sent Ted's sister Lena in England both the bill of sale and the deed for the meat market. In the accompanying letter, Ted said it was meant to repay the money that he had borrowed over the years.

The decision not to return to Glidden, a secret known only to the couple and their few Vancouver friends, was reached just days before the Bates left for Saskatchewan. Provincial relief authorities had contacted the local Salvation Army and arranged for the agency to cover the cost of the train fare for the family to Glidden. The tickets reportedly cost over one hundred dollars. The day before they were scheduled to leave, the Bates sold all their remaining furniture and used the meagre proceeds to reclaim the ring and watch they had pawned earlier. They also bought a blue reefer coat for Jackie for the Saskatchewan winter. It's debatable how much the boy was told by his parents or figured out on his own. On his last day at school, he simply told his teacher, "Well, that's the last apple you'll get Miss McKay. We are leaving for the prairies tomorrow."[24]

On 29 November, the Bates family boarded a CN passenger train for the two-day trip to Saskatoon. As their luck would have it, there was one last hitch at the station: they had too much baggage. The agent, seeing that they were a relief case, grudgingly agreed to send their trunks on to Saskatchewan on the understanding that the extra shipping fee would have to be paid there. It was an irritating beginning to their trip home—one they didn't need. It was as if they were being reminded that they too were excess baggage, being shipped back to Saskatchewan in the hope that they would be claimed there. Slim Babcock, at the station to see them off, was struck by how the trip to Saskatchewan weighed heavily on the couple. They seemed to be in a stupor, as if they had been battered into submission. Rose appeared "downhearted ... very desperate ... I could see that she did not relish the idea of the return trip." She looked "like a prisoner going into an exile in hell."

Ted was equally despondent. Up until the last few weeks in Vancouver, he had usually been fairly upbeat, confident that one of the corner grocery stores would see them through the Depression. It was the same kind of optimism that had brought him to Glidden at the start of the 1920s. But those days were past. Ted Bates had been soundly defeated by the Depression, one of its many casualties. He may have tried to hide his true feelings that day, but the expression on his face, full of melancholy and self-doubt, gave him away. "He looked to me," Babcock declared, "like a man blown up by a shell, buried, and blown up again."[25]

CHAPTER THREE

THEY WON'T
HAVE US HERE

S askatoon billed itself as the "wonder city." In 1901, the former temperance colony on the banks of the South
Saskatchewan River was just a sleepy hamlet of 113 people,
with no sidewalks, no sewers, no hospital, and no police or
fire protection. Ten years later, the population had sky-
rocketed to 12,000, thanks to the settlement boom and an aggressive
self-promotion. Even then, Saskatoon boosters angrily disputed the
1911 census figures and methodically conducted their own head count,
including people staying in hotels or passing through on trains, and, of
course, counting pregnant women as two.

Saskatoon's spectacular transformation seemed a sure sign that the
city was well along the road to greatness. Starry-eyed investors, out to
make a quick buck, certainly believed so. Between 1910 and 1913, 257 real
estate firms sold the equivalent of three Saskatoons of the size of the
one that exists today. In all, fifteen thousand acres, most of them no
more than gopher-riddled fields, were surveyed outside the 1911 city
limits—enough land to accommodate an estimated population of five
hundred thousand people, half the population of the province of
Saskatchewan in 2001.

"If there is one preeminent character in these western cities,"
wrote Edinburgh-born Elizabeth Mitchell, who visited Saskatoon

after graduating from Oxford in 1913, "it is the note of change, of rapid and amazing and unpredictable change. Towns rise like vapour from a river."[1] A writer for the *Toronto Globe* agreed. "At such a rate of speed," he conceded, "one dare not make any prediction as to what Saskatoon will not have done by a generation from now."[2]

These great expectations for the city had been long dashed by the time the Bates family arrived two decades later as relief refugees from Vancouver. The Saskatoon real estate bubble had been propelled skyward by grossly overinflated property values. When that bubble burst in 1912, the ever-ambitious city was on the hook for an incredible $7.6 million in debenture debt. It had not only recklessly poured millions of dollars into facilities and services not needed for the foreseeable future, but had blithely funded this development by borrowing money against unrealistic assessment rates.

For the next few decades, Saskatoon remained literally stuck in its development as it scrambled to reduce municipal services and cut spending. But any savings were effectively offset by hundreds of thousands of dollars in outstanding tax arrears. Indeed, Saskatoon was financially hobbled well before the Depression struck. This indebtedness would only grow in the early 1930s since relief payments were supposed to be funded in the first instance from municipal revenues. The city was consequently forced to borrow money to meet its relief obligations, while increasingly leaning on the province for emergency funds to avoid bankruptcy.

It also became mean-spirited and punitive in an effort to keep its relief rolls from ballooning. As of November 1932, a new relief application form gave Saskatoon officials the right to enter homes at any time, day or night, to ensure that recipients were truly destitute and not hiding luxury items, such as a radio. The form also required all relief disbursements to be repaid in full, by the confiscation of personal effects and property if necessary.

The Bates were only supposed to stay in Saskatoon long enough to change trains en route to Glidden. But when they disembarked at the Canadian National Railway station at 4 A.M. on Friday, 1 December 1933, Ted duly kept his promise to Rose and made some inquiries about obtaining work, or failing that, relief.

Things looked promising for a family down on its luck. Directly east of the train station, a luxurious, chateau-style railway hotel, named the Bessborough in honour of Canada's governor-general, now rose from the banks of the South Saskatchewan River. A few hundred yards to the south, the new Broadway Bridge linked Saskatoon's south downtown with the original Nutana settlement on the east side of the river. Surely, there should be some kind of work for Ted. But the projects were a false indicator of the city's economic health. Although the grand brick and stone exterior of the Bessborough Hotel had been completed by the fall of 1931, Saskatoon's castle on the river sat empty and silent while CN waited for the return of better times before finishing the interior. The hotel would not open until December 1935.

The construction of the $850,000 Broadway Bridge, on the other hand, had provided only short-term employment to some of the twenty-four hundred married men who had registered for relief at the start of the Depression. Once the work was done, the city began actively encouraging families to take out pioneer farms in the province's middle north under a new federal settlement program. One of the new settlements in the bush near Loon Lake was imaginatively named Little Saskatoon, where former city dwellers traded one kind of poverty for another. The Bates, if they had lived in Saskatoon, might have been among them.

By mid-morning, Ted and Rose, with Jackie in tow, had made their way to the Church of the Nazarene on Avenue G South to see Reverend Thomas Bunting about a referral to the local relief office. Bunting often represented the unemployed in their dealings with the city and was hired by the provincial government the following year to help get Saskatoon families settled on farms. After Ted recounted the sorry circumstances that had brought them back to Saskatchewan, Bunting asked why they hadn't continued on to Glidden. Rose replied that they had decided to stay over because Jackie was sick. A concerned Bunting offered to get a doctor, but Rose said the boy would be fine once he got a good rest, even if it meant pawning the last of her jewellery to pay for a room.

Ted then raised the matter of relief. He told Bunting that "it was the hardest thing to do ... to go back to Glidden" and wondered whether it would be possible to remain in Saskatoon. He had "lost everything in Vancouver" and was "distressed" at the prospect of returning as a relief case to the village where he was "so well known."[3] But all the minister could offer the family, since they had never been residents, was his help in getting temporary assistance to carry them through the weekend.

Bunting knew from his caseload that he couldn't get them any more support. There were already too many local people calling on the limited resources the civic relief board had to offer. In fact, that very same day the city suspended support for all single unemployed people, including those who may have been born in Saskatoon and lived there all their lives. Besides, it was not as if the Bates were stranded in Saskatchewan's second largest city. They had train tickets to Glidden where at least they could obtain relief, no matter how embarrassing it might be. Other families faced grimmer prospects.

At the end of their interview, Reverend Bunting telephoned G. W. Parker, the city relief officer, and asked for temporary assistance to carry the family through to Monday when the next train left for Glidden. He was flatly turned down. "They don't take everybody with open arms," is how Bunting summed up the attitude of city relief officials.[4] That was an understatement. According to a report in the local newspaper, Parker wanted to hire a security guard to protect his staff. Irate relief applicants, who had been turned away, had not only verbally abused relief officers, but had thrown ink wells, telephones, and anything else within reach on the desks.

Undeterred, Reverend Bunting took Ted to see Murray McIntyre, a member of the local relief board, and presented the family's case. McIntyre agreed to the request and told Bates to go to the city relief office, while he called ahead about the matter. By the time Ted arrived there that afternoon, relief officials had already been briefed about the situation and were ready to provide help for the weekend only. But Ted didn't want to go to Glidden on Monday morning and tried his best to convince assistant relief officer J. J. McGrath that his family should be able to stay in Saskatoon. McGrath waved away the request by asking how they were fixed for meals that day and if they had a place to stay. Ted responded that they had eaten lunch, probably thanks to Bunting, and would be okay for the rest of the day. He also said they had money for a hotel room that night. McGrath then handed him a voucher for two nights' accommodation, the Saturday and Sunday, at the Western Hotel on 2nd Avenue South. He also gave him a ticket with fifteen neatly punched holes for meals at the Ovleda Café at 236 20th Street West: two each on Saturday and Sunday and one each for Monday, the day they were expected to leave.

McGrath later reported that Ted appeared satisfied with what he had been given. "He got what he asked for," is how the relief official tersely put it.[5] And he was right—to a certain extent. The city was under no obligation to provide any assistance since the Bates shouldn't have stopped over in Saskatoon but continued on to Glidden that same morning, despite Jackie's apparent illness. That's probably why Ted never complained about his family's treatment. He knew they were fortunate to get any help, if only for a few days. Relief officials could have sat on their hands, insisting that the family was not their responsibility. Instead, the city accommodated the Bates as best it could under the circumstances. The sooner they left Saskatoon, the better. They were not to be placed on the civic relief rolls, nor could they expect any more assistance beyond Monday morning. They had to go home.

What no one appreciated, however, is that the offer of temporary relief actually came as a cruel blow to the Bates, hammering in the fact that there would be no long-term relief or any chance of staying in Saskatoon. Bunting, McIntyre, and McGrath, upon hearing the reason for the family's return to Saskatchewan, innocently assumed they were doing them a favour at a time of personal crisis. Ted, Rose, and especially their sick little boy could rest in relative comfort for a few days at the city's expense and then be on their way. It could be argued that Saskatoon handled the case with understanding and compassion.

But despite the city's help, Ted and Rose really meant it when they said that they didn't want to return to Glidden. Ted's reluctance to face his former friends and neighbours wasn't just another Depression story, intended to win over the sympathy of Saskatoon relief officials. He may have had tickets to Glidden in his pocket, but his family was not going to get on the train come Monday morning. It is almost certain that Ted had promised Rose that they would never go back to the village, and it was one promise he knew he had to keep. She wouldn't have come this far if she had had any doubts about the pledge he had made to her in Vancouver. Ted had given her plenty of reason in the past to question his sincerity, but this time Rose could count on him. He had been worn down by the Depression to the point where any fight had gone out of him.

Early Friday evening, the Bates checked into the Western Hotel. They paid for their room that first night, knowing that their relief voucher was good for only Saturday and Sunday. They probably used what little money remained from the sale of their furniture in Vancouver. It was an expense they really could not afford, but from their perspective it was better than being in Glidden.

While Jackie slept, his parents decided on their next move. There's no record of what they said to one another or whether they argued about what to do. It's not hard to imagine, though, the turmoil and anxiety in the room as they faced a road to the future that they didn't want to take. Clearly, the relief system had boxed them in, leaving them with only one option if they wanted help. But for Ted and Rose, already burdened with personal failure and the disgrace of needing relief, returning to Glidden was a dead end. The loss of dignity would become even more pronounced if they went back to the village, and that was something neither one of them had the inner strength to deal with.

There had to be something else they could do—but what? Going back to England was not a possibility, nor were they interested in joining the thousands of farm families starting over again in the province's forest fringe. They could have tried to survive by eking out a marginal existence in another urban centre in the province. Migrants from rural areas, for example, had made Prince Albert the fastest-growing city in western Canada in the first half of the 1930s. It would have been difficult, but not impossible, to get by in one of Saskatchewan's cities. If they supported themselves for a year, they could then apply for relief. But that too was apparently never considered. It seems that the Bates' hard-luck experience in Vancouver had robbed them of any remaining confidence that they could make a go of it somewhere else. They had run out of hope when they needed it the most.

The other possible solution was for the pair to go their separate ways, with one of them taking Jackie. That was something that Rose had wanted to do when her relationship with Ted was foundering on the rocks and she was ready to abandon him to his slovenly ways. But he had refused to let the child go, and Rose certainly wasn't going to be the one to do so this time. Jackie made their dysfunctional marriage tolerable, brightening their otherwise bleak lives. And since neither Ted nor Rose was willing to give their son up, they were prepared to stay together, even though any love that once burned between them had long since been snuffed out.

So, what *were* the Bates going to do? For Rose, there was only one answer to their predicament, a kind of final solution to their Depression odyssey: take their own lives and that of Jackie. She had openly talked about suicide in her letter to Ted's sister in 1932 and also repeatedly threatened in Vancouver to kill herself rather than go back to Glidden. That time now seemed to have arrived. It was staring her in the face.

Ted, for his part, was normally not the kind of person who would entertain such thoughts. He enjoyed life too much. But he went along with Rose that fateful night in the Saskatoon hotel room, as he had repeatedly done over the past few months. After all, she was the one who had pushed for the sale of the meat market. She was the one who had wanted to start over in Vancouver. And she was the one who had refused to go back to Glidden, at any cost. The Depression had chewed Ted up and spat him out. He was ready to give up and would probably have agreed to anything if it promised a way out of their mess. Ending their lives must have seemed the only sensible course of action, especially when he saw no future for them.

This profound sense of desolation that weighed down on Ted and Rose, as if they were helplessly trapped in a pressure chamber, was not uncommon in Saskatchewan during the Depression. Others felt it too. The desperate times spawned any number of desperate acts. They all had one thing in common: lives were irreparably damaged, if not forever destroyed. Tom Sukanen, a Finnish immigrant who had homesteaded near Macrorie, spent the decade building an ocean-going ship that he intended to sail all the way back home. He suffered a breakdown while hauling the vessel to the Saskatchewan River and later died in the Battleford asylum. Today, Sukanen's ship is on display at a small museum outside Moose Jaw. Edna Weber, meanwhile, was only sixteen in September 1937 when her parents sold her into marriage to a farmer thirty years older. Her father reportedly told the dust-bowl bride, "If you do this thing, it will help all of us ... they'll be one less mouth to feed here."[6] These people were looked upon, both then and now, as the unfortunate victims of the Depression, of the carnage wrought by the double whammy of depressed prices and devastating drought. It was a way of making sense of what had happened during the 1930s, without necessarily justifying it.

In the case of the Bates, they not only had to contend with inflexible relief policies, but also their own headstrong pride, something that many Canadians struggled to overcome at the time. "It is this stiff-back sense of pride," author Pierre Berton observed in *The Great Depression*, "that comes through again and again in the stories of those who were forced by circumstances to accept relief."7 That much is perfectly understandable. Ted and Rose were too ashamed to return to Glidden in need of relief and chose to end their lives instead. But why did Jackie have to die with them? Why kill an innocent eight-year-old boy?

That's what made the Bates' behaviour so abhorrent. They were prepared to carry out a murder, not just of anyone, but of their own son. Such an unthinkable act cannot simply be blamed on the Depression or their pride, unless one unquestionably accepts the argument that the distress at the thought of going back to the village as a relief case blinded their judgment. Ted and Rose had fallen into an intoxicated, Depression-induced stupor, not really knowing what they were doing—hence the cold-blooded decision to take their young child's life with theirs.

This reading of the situation, however, misses one other key consideration: the couple's strained marriage and how it undoubtedly clouded their thinking that night. The Bates were unhappy partners in a marriage held together by their struggle over their only child. Giving Jackie up was impossible for both of them, so in their selfishness, Ted and Rose decided that the boy had to die too rather than be left alone in the world. They believed that Jackie would be better off together with his parents in death than facing the future as an orphan. Here was the real victim.

The other matter Ted and Rose had to sort out, once they had reached their decision, was how they were going to kill themselves and Jackie. There was any number of ways. The newspapers carried stories almost daily about how people from across the West had died by their own hand. The toll could also be counted on tombstones in rural cemeteries, especially those graves around the perimeter or just beyond the graveyard fence. People turned guns on themselves, slashed their wrists, drank poison, or broke their necks at the end of a rope. Some suicide attempts went terribly wrong. One hapless individual tied a thin electrical cord around his neck, only to have it break when he jumped from a chair. He was later found in bed, dead from an apparent heart attack, with the cord still wrapped around his neck. Even when loved ones intervened, it was sometimes too late. A farm wife, admitted to the North Battleford Mental Hospital by her family, found release by consuming gopher poison during a visit home.

Rose wanted to use potassium cyanide, a powerful respiratory inhibitor, in some kind of deadly cocktail, but Ted convinced her that death by carbon monoxide gas would be more peaceful. They would just fall asleep with their son and never wake up. It's uncertain where he got the idea from. Two days before the Bates arrived in Saskatoon, newspapers carried the sad account of an elderly Ontario couple whose decomposed bodies were found by police several days after an unlighted gas jet on their stove was left on in their home. The coroner's jury requested that a canary be placed in the dwelling under identical circumstances to see whether it too would succumb to the fumes. Ted could have read the story and suggested doing something similar— only this time on purpose.

The next morning, after a long, sleepless night, Ted and Rose began to put their plan into action. They started with letters. Maybe they believed that putting down on paper what they intended to do would prevent them from changing their minds. It would effectively force them to carry through with their suicides and might have been a way of justifying their actions after their deaths. That they wrote letters, though, indicated that their decision to kill themselves and Jackie was not an impulsive act; they had not suddenly been overcome with shame on their way to Glidden and looked for a way to end their lives.

No, their death pact was a carefully calculated scheme.

The first letter, on Western Hotel stationery and dated and mailed that same day, was written to their former Vancouver chum, Slim Babcock. Ted began by briefly outlining what had happened after their arrival in Saskatoon—"we have got to go on to Glidden on Monday"—and then offered a somewhat circuitous account of what they planned to do. "So if you don't hear from us again you will know we never arrived," he wrote, "but we will all meet again sometime I hope so don't think to bad of us if anything should happen and be good to yourself."[8] Babcock knew that the Bates had left Vancouver resolved never to go back to Glidden, but whether he would have guessed what the cryptic note was hinting at is another matter.

Ted sent a similar letter to his former Vancouver landlord, Bob Wolstone. "I went to see the relief people but have to go on to Glidden," he glumly reported, "They won't have us here."[9] Ted said little more except to advise Wolstone that he had left his two lucky coins above the bedroom door of their former apartment. He also enclosed a ticket for a raffle to be held on 8 December and told him to claim the prize if it happened to win.

Ted also penned a short letter to his good friend Stan Elliot, who had handled the sale of the meat market in Glidden. He had written Elliot three times from Vancouver that fall, imploring him to try to get the outstanding balance from the sale of the store to the Warman family. This time, without a single word of explanation, Ted informed his former neighbour that he had surrendered the bill of sale and certificate to the Glidden property to his sister, Lena, in England. "I told her you was an agent," he advised Elliot, "so I guess she will get in touch with you sometime. We was coming back to Glidden but changed our mind."[10] Ted ended the note with holiday wishes.

His last letter was to his mother. Not knowing what to say or how to say it, Ted wished her a Merry Christmas and then added that she was not to write until she had heard from him again.

Later in the afternoon, after their first "relief" meal at the Ovledo Café, the family trooped over to the Allan Service Station, less than two blocks east at the corner of 20th Street West and Avenue A. Allan Bernbaum, one of the co-proprietors and a mechanic, was working that day when the trio arrived. Ted introduced himself before asking about renting a car, especially a model that would keep the cold winter wind out. Bernbaum replied that he wasn't in the rental business but might be willing to make his own car available for the right price. Ted then recited the story that he had probably been practising in his head all morning. He said that his family had recently arrived from Vancouver, where he owned a grocery store and a car. He also claimed to have twenty-five hundred dollars in cash from selling their house and wanted to invest the proceeds in some farmland. The question was where. Bernbaum suggested that he head north, that there was good land around Rosthern. Ted agreed to investigate the district and wondered about other areas, particularly to the west. Rose even joined in the conversation, even though she had never shown any interest in farming before.

Because of the cold, the Bates did not linger at the service station but said they would come back the next day or possibly Monday. Bernbaum indicated he might have a car for them, but left it at that. Nothing was mentioned about what it would cost. As they were about to leave, he asked about Jackie, who looked noticeably pale and sickly. Rose told him that her son had suffered fainting spells since birth. Ted added that they sometimes gave him brandy and thought they should probably get some at the nearby liquor store.

Curiously, Harry Vossberg, the manager at the Western Hotel, had a completely different recollection of Jackie during the family's stay in Saskatoon. He remembered a happy little boy dropping off the key at the front desk each time the Bates went out and picking it up when they returned. It's quite likely that Jackie looked upon their time in the hotel as an adventure, while the visit to the service station meant they would be on the move yet again. The boy had to know from listening to the conversations over the past few days that he would not be going back to Glidden, would not be seeing his old school friends, if his parents had their way.

He should also have realized that something else was amiss. One day, his parents were asking a Saskatoon minister to help them secure relief assistance, the next day they were talking to a garage operator about sinking twenty-five hundred dollars into a Saskatchewan farm. It's no wonder that he seemed ill while they made arrangements to hire a car to take them to who knew where.

Sadly, though, Jackie Bates may have been the only person in Saskatoon who had some inkling that all was not right with his parents. Although civic relief authorities had extended a helping hand, their main concern was that the Bates be on their way Monday morning. They had no interest in listening to Ted and Rose's complaints that they did not want to go back to Glidden. And who was to say that Ted and Rose were not bearing up well given the circumstances that had brought them back to Saskatchewan? Reverend Bunting and relief officer McGrath had come into contact with all kinds of people who had been warped in some way by the Depression. On the surface at least, it appeared as though the couple was resigned to their fate. Otherwise, why didn't they make a bigger fuss about going home to Glidden?

The Bates' pride evidently cut two ways. They were too ashamed to return to the village yet they didn't want to cause a public commotion over being sent back. Ted and Rose also gave no outward indication that anything was wrong once they had decided on their suicide scheme. The hotel manager, who saw the Bates over the course of several days, regarded his guests as "very nice people, very quiet."[11] It was a view shared by everyone who came into contact with the family that weekend. All said they appeared "normal." Not even Rose's gaunt appearance raised any eyebrows, which was not surprising given the toll that the Depression had taken on people's health.

Nor did Allan Bernbaum suspect that they were lying about their situation. When the Bates returned to the service station on the Sunday afternoon, he talked at length with Ted about land and live-stock, while Rose and Jackie looked on. This certainly wasn't the behaviour of a couple bent on ending their lives along with that of their son. If Bernbaum had any doubts about the sincerity of the couple, he would not have agreed to make his car available to them Monday morning as they requested.

That Sunday night, their last in Saskatoon, Ted and Rose finalized their plan. They would pawn a few belongings in the morning and then use the money to rent Bernbaum's car. They had told him that they needed the vehicle for the day to look at farmland. In reality, they intended to drive to a secluded place somewhere in the country and leave the car running, confident that the carbon monoxide gas would kill them in their sleep.

Before heading out of the city, though, they had to deal with the three trunks that had been sent from Vancouver as excess baggage. They could have simply left them in storage at the Saskatoon station and thus avoided paying the shipping charges from the coast. It would have made no difference to their plan whether the trunks were claimed or not. But Ted and Rose were apparently not comfortable with the idea that some of their belongings—in effect, part of their life— would be left behind in Saskatoon. They were resolved to tie up any loose ends before facing death, and that included retrieving the trunks and sending them to their Vancouver friends, Ruby and Frank Gardiner.

It fell to Rose to write the Gardiners that the three trunks were being shipped to them collect. Her letter, undated as was her habit, was written sometime late Sunday night or early Monday morning, only hours before the couple left on their death trip. "Well I hope you are fine and flourishing," she began. "Gee its enough to freeze the balls off a brass monkey here, well we are taking the liberty with you this time old palls. We are sending our D— boxes back in your name today as we would rather you have them than any other sucker. I only wish we had left them all with you in the start but we didn't and <u>thats that</u>." Rose then apologized for returning the trunks collect and suggested that the Gardiners could recover the cost of paying for them by selling some of the contents. "I hope you will be able to rais the dough to get them," she wrote, "as there is lots you can make use of."

If the letter had ended there, there would have been no record of the anguish and torment that gripped Rose. But she could not keep silent and hinted, albeit obliquely, at what she and Ted were about to do: "When you go through them [trunks] will you burn all traces of us you may come across and mums the word to all what one dont know wont hurt one will it." She then cried out in a plaintive voice as if she faced her imminent death, "I cant stand the pressure of it all so we will sleep it off or try I am going to get tight as a fool and make the old boy ditto to keep is pecker up. So good by dear palls till we meet again with fond love and happy thoughts of the many laughs we have had."[12] The letter to the Gardiners was mailed Monday morning, 4 December, after the Bates had checked out of the hotel. They said nothing to the clerk about where they were going. They simply set off with two small suitcases for the Ovledo Café for their last meal on the city. Somewhere after breakfast, Rose sold a coat at a second-hand store and jewellery at another. They didn't have to go out of their way. There was a pawn shop near the restaurant and another next door to the garage. The items fetched $12.

It was 9:30 A.M. by the time they reached the Allan Service Station. Bernbaum was busy getting his car ready for them: a grey 1929 Chevrolet coach, with Saskatchewan plate number 16-511. Bernbaum asked for $10 for use of the automobile for the day. He also warned them that there was only about two gallons of gas in the tank and that they would need more for their trip. Rose paid him $12.20 for the rental and six gallons of fuel. Ted then chimed in that they preferred not to put down a deposit for the car so that they might have enough money on hand for any land they might find. Bernbaum saw no problem with that. He also made no objection when Ted said they might keep the car an extra day. He was so trusting of the Bates and their story that he only glanced at Ted's British Columbia driver's licence and never even asked where they were staying in Saskatoon.

Since it was another frigid day, Bernbaum put an old blanket and cowhide robe in the car. He wanted to give more to keep them warm during their drive, but the Bates told him they had blankets of their own back at their hotel. He also expressed concern about Ted, who appeared uncomfortably cold in his light overcoat, but his worry was answered with the explanation that Ted had left his fur coat in his trunk at the train station, just a block away, and that they were headed there next to retrieve it.

The Bates left the service station in Bernbaum's car shortly before 11 A.M. Ted drove over to the Union Baggage Transfer office and went inside alone to claim the trunks from Vancouver. The charges totalled $4.45, including a storage fee of 45 cents per item. No sooner had Ted paid the bill than he told the manager, J. T. Keyser, that he wanted the three trunks sent right back, this time collect, to Mr. and Mrs. F. Gardiner. This request undoubtedly seemed a little strange, if not bizarre, but Ted was ready with a new lie. He told Keyser that he had come to Saskatoon to take a job, and when it didn't work out he decided to return to Vancouver. Ted accompanied a CN truck driver over to the freight shed with the trunks and was then taken back to the car. "He did not say anything on this trip," Herb Ashton remembered. "He seemed a very nice man but very quiet."[13]

It was just past noon when the Bates finally left Saskatoon. But instead of driving north to Rosthern as they told Bernbaum, Ted headed out Highway 14, a gravelled road which ran due west from the city. They were driving in the general direction of Glidden, but Highway 7 through Rosetown and Kindersley would have been a more direct route even if it was little more than a dirt road. Maybe Ted thought that Rose would change her mind and realize that going to Glidden was better than taking their lives. He certainly seemed to be having second thoughts. He had evidently told Rose that she and the boy should pass out first from the gas and that he would follow.

Jackie was blissfully reading in the back seat of the car. His parents had bought him two new Big Little Books, *Mickey Mouse the Mail Pilot* and *Chester Gump at Silver Creek Ranch*, for the trip.[14] They probably wanted to keep him occupied so that he didn't ask difficult questions like "Where are we going?" and "What are we going to do when we get there?"

As it was, it was a good thing that he was absorbed in the books, for Rose wanted her husband to pull off the road as soon as they were out of Saskatoon. Ted insisted that they had to wait until it was dark. It didn't seem to occur to them that they should try to find a spot somewhere on the outskirts of Saskatoon and wait out the day to ensure that there was still enough gas in the tank to fulfill their deadly plan.

By mid-afternoon the Bates had reached Perdue, a product of the settlement boom and the CPR, about forty-four miles from Saskatoon. There was a certain irony to the name, which was selected in 1908 to recognize a Winnipeg doctor. "Perdu" in French means lost, and that certainly applied to the Bates as they anxiously searched for an end to their troubles and a way out of the Depression. For the time being, they would settle for a cup of coffee and turned off the highway into the village. The first stop was the post office, where Ted mailed another letter to the Gardiners, this one containing the bill of lading for the three trunks. He also posted the note he had written to Stan Elliot over the weekend, explaining that they were not coming back to Glidden. This delay in sending the letter was another sign that Ted had his doubts about their suicide plan. Now, though, there seemed to be no turning back.

The family slipped into the King George Café, run by Der Ying. Rose found a seat by the heater and sat there smoking, staring out the window, while sipping her coffee absent-mindedly. Jackie was at the table with her and had something to eat while he read one of his new books. Ted, however, couldn't stay still and anxiously stood at the counter with his coffee as if he were waiting for something to happen. Ying asked Ted where they were from and when told it was Vancouver, chatted with him about the city. He also wanted to know where they were going. Ted simply replied, "About fifteen miles."[15]

About 3 P.M., Alcide Belliveau, the village barber, came into the café to buy some cigarettes. He knew right away that the family were strangers, said hello, and then went on his way through the kitchen and out the back door to have a smoke. Ted followed him outside and walked around for a few moments, drawing heavily on his cigarette, before turning back to Belliveau and asking, "Is there any empty buildings around here that a man could use?" The barber, noticing that Ted wasn't wearing a coat suited for the weather, asked him how far he wanted to go. Ted replied it didn't matter. Belliveau directed him to an empty shack west of town on the right-hand side of the highway. Ted buttoned up the top of his coat as if he were preparing for the worst, and declared, "God damn it, a man has to do something."[16] He then threw his cigarette on the ground and headed back inside to get Rose and Jackie.

CHAPTER FOUR

LET'S GO IN HERE
AND FINISH IT

The Eagle Hills don't look anything like the Saskatchewan of the popular imagination. Running from the Battle River near the Battlefords southeast to Highway 14 between Perdue and Biggar, they are part of the Missouri Couteau escarpment. Millions of years ago, the underlying bedrock was thrust upward along a fault line. Then, a series of glaciers deposited a mantle of drift or till, sometimes several hundred yards in depth.

The hills were formed during a period of so-called ice stagnation when the great Laurentide ice sheet began to withdraw some ten to twelve thousand years ago. Debris melted out along the retreating face of the glacier to give birth to a series of steep, rolling moraines. Today, the landscape is often described as hummocky or undulating. But for anyone who has travelled through the hills, "roller-coaster" would be a more fitting term. Great vistas, offering million-dollar views, alternate with deep, at times heavily wooded, ravines.

Unlike most other Saskatchewan places, the hills have been known for generations by a Cree name, the phrase *mikisiw waciy* (eagle hills), in recognition of the eagles that nested in the area. They were a popular camping place for the Blackfoot, Gros Ventre, Assiniboine, and Cree who spent several months each year hunting and trapping in the area, especially during the winter.

Fur traders followed in the eighteenth century. Anthony Henday (1754) and Matthew Cocking (1772), both Hudson's Bay Company men, travelled through the uplands with their Indian escorts as part of their investigations to determine how and where the interior trade was being siphoned away by its Montreal-based competitors. Part of the answer was Fort Montagne d'Aigle, also known as Eagle Hill Fort, along the northern edge of the hills.

Come the nineteenth century, First Nations and mixed-blood groups increasingly turned to the plentiful game resources of the hills as the great bison herds were hunted to near extinction. The father of the famed Cree chief Big Bear often pitched his skin lodge in the area. In the 1870s, three Nakota bands (Grizzly Bear's Head, Lean Man, and Mosquito) and one Cree band (Red Pheasant) were deposited on reserves in the northwest part of the hills so that they would not interfere with agricultural settlement to the south. The rolling, timbered landscape suited traditional pursuits like hunting and gathering, but it proved poor farmland at a time when the federal government expected Indians to begin to raise crops to feed themselves.

Both the CPR and Grand Trunk Pacific (the forerunner of CN) laid steel through the district in 1908, deliberately skirting the southern edge of the hills. Several sections were officially classified by surveyors as "non-agricultural," prompting Ottawa to set aside three blocks of land to form the Keppel Forest Reserve (named in honour of a British admiral in the Royal Navy).[1] Homesteaders, however, were willing to take the gamble, especially when it cost only a ten-dollar registration fee for the chance to own 160 acres. They moved into the region, almost by default, when more promising areas were no longer available. Some even requested land in the forest reserve.

Those who first settled the Eagle Hills generally found it to be an impoverishing experience, all the more so because of the difficulties of teasing a crop from the gravelly, if not sandy, terrain. Several abandoned their holdings before meeting their homestead obligations and moved on to other locations or simply gave up. It was not uncommon for the same parcel of land to be occupied by a succession of would-be wheat kings. The farmers who persisted in breaking the tough prairie wool and cultivating the hills were stubborn, rarely lucky, and somehow managed to hang on. A few homesteaders grazed cattle, which seemed a more appropriate use of the land, or worked at other jobs to supplement their meagre farm income. Most families also relied on local game, especially deer, much like the Indians who once hunted bison that had sought shelter from winter's biting winds in the coulees.[2]

Ted and Rose Bates were also in search of refuge when they turned off Highway 14 in the dying light of the late afternoon sun of Monday, 4 December 1933, and headed north on what is now known as Centre Road into the Eagle Hills. Their route was several miles from the place that the Perdue barber had mentioned earlier that afternoon during their stop for coffee. The Bates were likely worried that the abandoned building was too close to the highway, that they might be seen, and decided to push on and find something more isolated. The hills seemed a better alternative. Their car might not be found for days.

The road north was narrow, winding, and extremely rough from the packed snow. It would have been a difficult drive in the approaching darkness, and Ted had to be careful not to slide into the ditch while looking for a place to fulfill their suicide pact. Jackie, who no longer had enough light to read in the back seat, probably wondered where they were and where they were going. It certainly didn't seem as if the road led anywhere, unless it was a shortcut that his dad had heard about.

Archie Evanoff was sitting by his kitchen window when he heard the sound of a car approaching from the south at around dusk. The Russian immigrant had come to Perdue with his wife and young family in 1913 and took out a homestead in the hills. His skills as a hunter helped them survive their first years on the land. The family larder was usually filled with rabbits, ducks, geese, and venison. But in 1922, they headed to San Francisco where Archie plied his trade as a tinsmith. That lasted until 1926, when the family returned to Canada—ironically, to the same farm—in the hope that the booming wheat economy meant better times. The Great Depression imposed a different future.

Evanoff watched as the Bates' car turned left just a few yards south of his house and proceeded west over an old trail across one of his fields. He lost sight of the vehicle after it crested a hill, but expected it to come back in a matter of minutes because there was a gate across the trail on the west side of his property. Evanoff waited for some time, growing increasingly curious, before deciding to go in search of the mystery car. He cut across the field to the top of the hill and in the darkness initially mistook a pair of grazing horses for the vehicle. He then made his way down to the gate where the car would have been forced to stop, but could find no sign that it had come that far. Evanoff was headed back to the hill when he came across some tire tracks going down a steep ravine, filled by a large, frozen slough. He could see that the driver had tried getting the vehicle out by cutting across the face of the ravine, but that the car had evidently slid sideways into some thick brush lining the slough. He stood motionless, holding his breath, and listened for any noise coming from the ravine—he heard nothing. He then peered into the blackness below but could not make out the car, only a tangle of bush.

A puzzled Evanoff decided to walk the quarter mile back home and figure out what to do. But before he reached his place, he heard an engine racing from the other side of the hill. Minutes later, the car came bouncing along the trail. Evanoff waited by his gate, expecting the relieved occupants of the vehicle to stop and ask for directions. But when the car reached the road, the driver veered north and sped past him as if he weren't standing there. Maybe, he thought, they didn't see him. Evanoff looked on as the car turned at the next road to the left, the entrance to the Avalon school. Here, the driver circled the schoolyard, flashed the car

lights on the buildings, and then returned to the dirt road and continued north.

Evanoff didn't know what to make of the episode. What was the
crazy driver looking for on a cold December day in the middle of
nowhere? He knew that the strange car wasn't from the district, since
few people owned vehicles and those who did usually put them away
during the harsh winter months. If the people in the car were lost, as
they surely seemed to be, then why didn't they ask for help? Something
was peculiar, and Evanoff scurried off to see his neighbour, Pete
Horbenko, a fellow Russian immigrant who was renting a farm just
north of the school, to tell him about the incident and ask whether
he'd seen the car as well.

The Bates, in the meantime, drove north along the bumpy road
towards Louvain, named in honour of the Belgian medieval town
destroyed by the German army during the Great War. What they'd
been doing in Evanoff's pasture is not clear. Maybe Ted turned off
the road to get away from any farmhouses and curious people, or perhaps he assumed that the trail might lead to an abandoned building
where they could carry out their plan. Whatever the reason, getting
stuck in the ravine had been an upsetting experience for Ted and Rose,
already burdened with the knowledge of what they were about to do.
And the revving of the car's engine, in order to get out of the deep
hole, had used up precious gasoline. They had already travelled more
than sixty miles from Saskatoon on about eight gallons of gas, and
the gauge indicated they were getting low on fuel. They had to find
some. That's why they stopped briefly at the Avalon school, thinking
it was a house.

Two miles north, the Bates pulled into the yard of the Lee family.
It was almost 6 P.M. and already dark. Their random choice of a farmhouse was doubly fortunate. Like them, John Thomas (Jack) Lee was
from England and had immigrated to Canada in 1911; his wife and
daughter followed on his heels the next year. Lee was also one of the

few farmers in the area with a car, an old Ford, and might be willing to part with some gasoline.[3]

Lee popped his head out of his door as Ted and Rose were getting out of the car and asked the couple what they wanted. Ted said they were lost and wanted to know where they were. Lee, who had a wry sense of humour, replied that he knew where they were but wanted to know where they were going. Ted told him they were headed for Biggar and then on to Rosetown and needed some gas. Lee, though, was reticent to give some away, since he had only a little left in his own car. At this point, Rose spoke up and asked whether they could please buy a gallon of gas. Lee paused for a moment, maybe even glanced at Jackie watching from the back seat of the car, and then said, "Well if you are afraid you haven't got enough to get to Biggar, I will, sure."[4]

He grabbed his coat and a flashlight and went to his garage. While Lee drained gas into a container, Ted wanted to know whether he was on relief. Lee said no, but couldn't speak for the future, especially if prices and growing conditions didn't get any better soon. Ted talked a bit about farming, almost wistfully, suggesting that Lee was better off on the land where at least he could raise some animals and have something to eat. Lee didn't attach any significance to what Ted was musing about, nor should he have. The two of them, as he later recalled, were just making conversation while getting gas for the car. But clearly, Ted seemed to be reflecting on his life and what little was left of it.

Ted helped Lee put almost a gallon of gas into the coach and then asked how much he owed. Lee said thirty cents, but insisted that his family first come in the house and warm up before paying him. He knew from Ted's shaking while holding the flashlight that he was cold, and his wife and kid probably were too. He could also see that Ted didn't have a warm enough coat for the weather. Inside, Mrs. Lee was holding supper for her husband and another visiting couple, the Hulls, who farmed nearby. Once introductions had been made, the Bates were invited to sit at the table and share their evening meal of canned chicken, sauerkraut, and potatoes. Ted and Jackie ate heartily, while a visibly chilled Rose turned down any food, preferring to sip a few cups of tea.

Over supper, the Bates reported that someone along Highway 14 had given them wrong directions, telling them to turn right, and that's how they ended up driving into the hills. It was not long, they confessed, before they got badly lost. They even disclosed that they got stuck in a deep ditch when trying to turn around on a narrow road. Ted blamed the accident on a slipping clutch on the car. Rose quickly added that they would have been fine. If need be, she suggested, they could have slept in the car with the engine running until someone found them. Lee warned her, though, that it would have been a dangerous thing to do because the carbon monoxide fumes could have killed them if they weren't careful.

The Bates also felt obliged to offer an explanation for what they were doing on the road. Here, their story came closer to the truth. They recounted how they had once owned a butcher shop in Glidden, had tried their luck in Vancouver, and were now back in Saskatchewan to try to start over again, provided they got the money that was still owed them from the sale of the store. It was as if Ted and Rose wanted to justify their actions one last time without really saying what they intended to do. They also seemed to be looking for some sympathy from fellow immigrants. Times were tough, they all agreed, and the Depression had effectively destroyed their dreams of a better life in Canada.

Once the meal was over and the dishes cleared, everybody sat around and visited for about fifteen minutes over their tea. They talked animatedly about the old country and shared remembrances of favourite places, especially Rose and Thomas Hull, who was also English. Then, just before 7 P.M., the Bates got ready to leave. They stood there, in their coats, chatting for another ten minutes before saying their thank-yous and goodbyes. The Bates' apparent hesitation to get back into their car and on the road again was understandable.

Indeed, going from the warm hospitality of the Lee home out into the cold winter air was heavy with symbolism for Ted and Rose. They were turning their backs to the world and about to take that last step over the precipice.

Lee thought Rose looked a little nervous that evening, but when he asked her if she was okay, she claimed that she had been shaken up by the rough road and that it was the kind of excitement she could do without. He also wondered about Ted, who upon getting up from the table "lit a cigarette and smoked it pretty fast, and then lit another."[5] Lee assumed that he might have been anxious about the drive ahead of them. Ted had looked intently at his watch upon entering the farmhouse and said he wanted to get to Biggar in good time that night before heading on to Rosetown and then Glidden the next day.

Lee went outside with the family, showed them which way was south, and then watched them drive away in the direction of the highway to Biggar. He assured them that he had filled the car with enough gas that they wouldn't get stranded along the way. It was a cold evening, but not frigid by prairie winter standards. The overnight low, based on meteorological data for Biggar, was around 7°F (-14°C). There was also a slight breeze from the west.

As they drove south, Ted and Rose said little, keeping their thoughts to themselves while watching the road ahead in the car lights. Jackie could see little from the back seat and soon grew sleepy from the motion of the car. The only noise was the occasional roar of the engine as Ted struggled with the slipping clutch to change gears. The couple knew that it was now or never—it was just a matter of where. That question seemed to be answered when they reached the Avalon school grounds, the same place they had checked out over an hour earlier.

"Come on," Ted urged his wife, as if they had some distasteful chore awaiting them. "Let's go in here and finish it."

Rose answered right away, "All right, come on. We'll get it over."[6]

Avalon, or School District No. 4077, had been established in 1919 to meet the educational needs of local children from a twenty-square-mile area. It was a typical one-room Saskatchewan rural school, where a steady succession of young, single female teachers juggled eight grades while trying to cope with the distractions of poor pay, inadequate facilities, and uneven attendance, not to mention the isolation. Cold weather and the cost of heating the building often kept the school closed from December to February. Children also stayed home to help with the fall harvest or to prevent the spread of communicable diseases. Avalon, for example, was closed for several weeks in 1928 because of the outbreak of a nasty skin rash. Students of all ages were consequently concentrated in the primary grades, and it was unusual for many to quit before completing grade eight.

The 24- by 32-foot wooden school building, with an attached coal shed, sat facing south on a small knoll on the west side of the road, or to the right as the Bates came south. The playground, immediately east of the school, had a set of swings and a new flagpole and see-saw erected by Archie Evanoff that very year. There were also two outhouses on lower ground to the north, more than 150 feet from the rear of the school. A small barn, about half the size of the school building, stood nearby. It was used by kids who came to school by horse. Horses were also kept there when church, a wedding, or some other special event was held in the school building. The entire lot was surrounded by a short barbed-wire fence with a gate along the southern perimeter.

Ted drove the coach behind the school and down a slight grade to the barn. If Jackie was still awake, he was probably told that it was too late to get all the way to Biggar and that they would have to spend the night in the car. The barn doors were wired shut. Ted had no difficulty getting them open, but he found that there was a one-foot sill across the base of the doorway that made it impossible to drive the vehicle inside. Even if the sill had not been there, the Bates would still have been out of luck. The stable entrance was less than six feet wide, too narrow for the car. Ted and Rose could have tried to find another building, but that would have meant more driving and wasting of gas. Instead, Ted backed up the car and drove around to the back, or west side, of the barn. He parked the vehicle facing north, as close to the wall as possible and turned off the engine.

Ted hoped that the car would be hidden from the road, or at least difficult to spot, especially since the barn's elevation was about six feet lower than the school's. The wind, though, was coming from the west that night and would have helped to dissipate any fumes from the engine. It would have been better for their purposes to have left the car on the east or sheltered side of the stable, even if it was not out of sight. As it was, they likely told Jackie that they would have some privacy by parking behind the barn and would not be disturbed during the night.

Once the car was in position, Ted and Rose dropped the front seat. They made a makeshift bed with the blankets that Allan Bernbaum had given them at the service station that morning in Saskatoon. They then got in the back with Jackie between them. Since she couldn't open her door easily, Rose climbed over her son to the rear passenger or right side, while Ted settled in on the boy's left. They shared the old hide robe to keep the cold away. Even though Jackie found himself in a strange place in the dark, it was the kind of moment when any child would have felt special. Lying under the blankets between his parents, he would have believed that everything was fine in the world and that no harm would come to him.

Ted and Rose didn't want to start the car engine until Jackie was fast asleep and they were a little more tired. Besides, their son had probably heard Jack Lee at supper warn about the dangers of sitting in an idling car in winter. It was best to wait. But their rest was soon disturbed by someone shouting at them. They had been found out!

The voices belonged to Archie Evanoff and two of his neighbours. Evanoff had been on his way back home after his visit with Peter Horbenko and was walking south when he spotted the phantom car again—this time behind the school. He hurried back to Horbenko's house and told him that the car they had both seen over an hour earlier had come back. The pair left right away for the school grounds, stopping to get another neighbour, Mark Nikitin, along the way. They probably wanted some extra help in case there was any trouble.

As the trio marched south along the road to the northeast corner of the school lot, they could see that the doors of the stables had been flung open. Horbenko, who held the contract as janitor for the school, immediately knew that something was odd. There had been a dance at the school the previous Thursday night and then the building had been closed until the new year. He had personally checked all the doors, including wiring up the door of the stable. When the men moved closer to investigate, they spied the front end of a car jutting out from behind the far side of the barn. They stopped, wondering what to do. Horbenko thought it might be a boy with a girl. But they didn't want to get any closer. One of the men instinctively yelled, "Hello, hello," several times. Then, the others started to holler, "Who are you? What do you want?"[7] Their shouting was so loud that Mrs. Nikitin, perched on her doorstep, eager for any more information about the mystery car, could hear their voices from over a half mile away. The men anxiously waited for a response, but no one answered. They stood there, huddled together, contemplating their next move. After about ten minutes, someone started the car. The roar of the engine in the cold evening air seemed to unnerve them, for they backed away and moved to the southeast corner of the grounds near the school gate.

After talking some more about what to do, they decided to leave the car alone and head home. But just then, the men saw two people coming towards them from the south. Thinking that they might be from the car, they yelled to them. To their surprise, it turned out to be Evanoff's seventeen-year-old son Nick and another neighbour, Irishman John O'Neill, who farmed nearby. The Evanoff family had become worried when Archie had been gone so long. No one else in

73

the house had seen the car that he'd spotted from the kitchen window and gone to look for. When Archie didn't come home after nearly two hours, Nick was sent to find his dad with the help of O'Neill. At the school, the pair was told about the car parked behind the barn and stole a look for themselves. Young Nick even shouted, but to no avail. Again, the men talked about what to do and again they came to the same conclusion: it was best to leave the matter until morning. They walked away, not realizing that if they had been able to overcome their fear about the car, they could have stopped a gruesome tragedy from unfolding.

Inside the car, Ted and Rose likely panicked when they heard the yelling and may even have argued about what they should do. If they waited quietly in the car, the men outside might have come closer to investigate, even opened the door to see if anyone was actually in the vehicle. And if they answered the cries, they would have had to explain their presence. Why were they parked there, seemingly hidden behind the school barn? Why didn't they ask to spend the night at a farmhouse in the area instead of sleeping in the car with their young son? The Bates had no other options except to start the car and see if that was enough to ward off the men. It seemed to have worked, for there was only one last isolated shout before everything felt silent again, except for the idling of the car.

Once the men had left, Ted and Rose lay back down with their son. It was probably no later than 9 P.M. It's not known whether Jackie had heard the commotion outside or what his parents might have said about it. The family just went to sleep, or at least tried to. "I thought of everything," remembered Rose, recalling when she lay there next to her boy with the engine running. "I fully realized what I was doing, and I prepared myself to meet the end."[8] All three soon lost consciousness.

By a fluke, the ground along the southwest corner of the barn was slightly higher. Whether Ted realized this or not when he parked the car along the building's western wall is debatable. It was dark, and the only light would have come from the headlights. But by positioning the vehicle to face north, the exhaust would have fed directly into a kind of pocket created by the higher ground to the south, the western wall of the barn, and the bottom of the car. The wind, blowing slightly from the west, would have helped gather the escaping carbon monoxide gas. Over time, it would have gradually seeped into the car interior, an invisible intruder intent on snuffing out the lives of the Bates family.

The grey Chevrolet coach was running for perhaps an hour. The gallon of gasoline that Jack Lee had been able to supply would not have kept the engine going for much longer. In fact, the fuel tank was almost empty when Rose was dragged from her sleep by Jackie's sharp coughing as he threw up a bit of supper. Ted was hacking and snorting too, trying to clear his throat and nose after puking all over his coat and down the side of the seat. Rose, confused and feeling sick herself from the smell of Ted's vomit and the exhaust fumes, managed to get up and shut the motor off. She then crawled unsteadily back under the covers.

Ted, Rose, and Jackie lay there for some time. It could have been several hours. When Rose finally emerged from her gas-induced haze, she could feel the cold all around her, but for a few moments she wasn't sure where she was. Then the realization hit her and she automatically turned to Jackie, asking him if he was okay. When he didn't answer, she reached for his hand. It was cold. Rose gently shook the boy, as if it would rouse him. But she was too late. Jackie was dead.

In one of the statements that Rose would give about the incident, she claimed to have "lost my reason for a time" upon finding the lifeless Jackie at her side.9 It's hard to contemplate the horror that shot through Rose as she realized that she and her husband had willingly murdered their own child. This was the same bright, eight-year-old boy who only hours earlier had gone to bed with his parents, happily looking forward to reading some more of his new Big Little Books the next morning. The same boy who Rose had once hoped would help salvage her marriage. The same boy who Rose had watched over so closely, as if he were the last thing in the world that mattered to her—and he was. Now, Jackie was gone, taken from her by her own hand, ironically at a time when she probably needed him the most.

Rose probably also thought about what had become of her life in Canada. The supper conversation with the Lees and Hulls had starkly reminded her of what she had left behind in England in order to come and live with Ted in Saskatchewan. It was bad enough that her husband had turned out to be such a rogue, but to land in godforsaken Glidden, with a wedding band on her finger, was like being sentenced to a life in purgatory. Even after she had managed to escape the dust bowl for Vancouver, they wanted to send her back to the village to stand before the people stripped of everything, especially her pride. For Rose, things seemed to have gone so tragically wrong in Canada, but in the end it was Jackie and not she who paid the price.

While Rose was coping with the shock of her son's death, she was body-slammed by another terrible thought—maybe Ted was dead too! She vigorously shook her husband's arm, willing him awake. "I was afraid he was dying," she recounted, "and I'd be left alone."[10]

Ted had survived, though only barely. Unlike poor little Jackie, his large body mass of 220 pounds should have afforded him greater protection from the carbon monoxide fumes. But Ted had been lying closest to the car exhaust and had sucked in more of the lethal fumes. When Rose finally managed to rouse him, he seemed to be in a deep trance and could hardly move his arms and legs. He just sat there in the dark, zombie-like, with vomit down his front and a trickle of blood running down the right corner of his mouth because he had bitten his tongue.

A frantic Rose pleaded with her husband, "Ted, I'm not going back without my boy. Do something! Finish me off too! I don't mind what you do."

Ted, however, couldn't think straight—everything for him was hazy—and plaintively replied, almost apologetically, "I don't know what to do."

"Do anything," she implored.

"But I only have a knife," he answered.

"That'll do," she declared.[11]

The couple sat there silently for a while with Jackie's cold body between them. They seemed to need some time to mourn his loss before ending their own lives. Besides, Ted was in rough shape and couldn't summon up the energy to harm anyone, even if he wanted to do it. Rose eventually said, "Come on, you'd better start."

Ted responded, "I can't."

Undeterred, she reached down and grabbed the car crank from the floor and waved it at him. "Crack me over the head with this crank," Rose instructed, "and when I pass out do it."

Ted asked in response, "What about me?"

By this point, Rose didn't care about her husband, didn't care about anything except joining Jackie in death. "You either do the same or fight it out," she told him.

Ted by now was equally resigned to his fate and calmly observed, "They can only hang me."[12]

While Ted tried to sharpen the blade of his penknife on the larger butcher knife that he carried with him, Rose got out some towels from their bag. She then leaned forward in her seat. Ted took the car crank and whacked her three times on the back of her head. "It hurt quite a bit," she later remembered, "but I did not pass out."[13] Any one of these blows from a person of Ted's build should have caused Rose to lose consciousness and perhaps even fractured her skull. After all, here was a man who dispatched steers with a hammer blow before butchering them. But the carbon monoxide gas had robbed him of any strength, and each hit from the crank glanced off Rose's head as if Ted were swinging in slow motion.

Even though Rose had been only momentarily stunned, she still wanted Ted to kill her. At her urging, he grasped the large butcher knife and held the point of its nine-inch blade over her chest, intent on plunging it deep into her heart. He couldn't, however, put any force behind the knife and dropped it to the floor. He then took his penknife and wildly slashed at her neck in the dark, while she pushed her head against the back seat so that she wouldn't flinch. But even that was too tiring for him, and he had to rest a short time before hacking at her neck again.

The thrusts of the penknife left a deep, jagged cut on the left side of Rose's neck. By a quirk of fate, Ted had missed her carotid artery by a fraction of an inch, or he would have been sharing the car with two dead bodies. He did manage, though, to completely sever her sternomastoid muscle, leaving a gaping hole from which blood oozed onto the collar of her coat. Rose never let out a scream or even a whimper during the attack, but calmly absorbed the feeble blows from the penknife as if they were penance for what she had done.

For the next few hours, while Ted dozed in and out of sleep, Rose sat there, bleeding from her neck. Although she had used three towels to soak up the blood, she realized that the wound was not fatal and that she would have to do something else if she wanted to end her life. Ted wished aloud that he had brought a gun along with them, a sentiment shared by Rose. "If we had had a gun," she later vowed, "we would have both ended it."[14]

Towards daylight, the morning of Tuesday, 5 December, the pair decided on a last course of action. They would slash their wrists and meet death that way. Each took a razor blade from Ted's shaving kit and pushed up their coat sleeves. Ted hesitated at first, asking Rose where he would find his pulse. She felt his wrist and admitted with some frustration, "I can't find it. Your hand is too fat, but I think it is here."[15]

Ted sliced his left wrist first, just above the thumb. He then realized that the cut was in the wrong place, so he cut the wrist a second

78

time before taking the blade in his other hand to do the right one. Rose followed suit, quickly cutting both wrists, but only superficially. The Bates dropped the razor blades on the floor of the car and then lay down in the back seat, with Jackie's cold body between them, waiting for death to take them too.

It wasn't supposed to happen this way. All three were to perish at the same time, carried off by carbon monoxide poisoning in a car that was to serve as their tomb. The family was to become just another Depression statistic, headline news for a day or two, and then forgotten. But the grim drama played out against the backdrop of the Avalon school in the Eagle Hills was headed for a different outcome. Someone was outside the car again, calling out to them and trying to peer through the frosted windows. There would be no escape for Ted and Rose.

CHAPTER FIVE

I KNOW
WE'LL HANG

Ted and Rose Bates were damn lucky to be alive. That was the candid assessment of Dr. William Brace. A Toronto-trained physician who had been practising in the Biggar district for almost two decades, Brace had seen his share of injuries, especially during his service overseas in the Canadian Medical Corps during the Great War. He consequently wasn't fazed when RCMP constable Donald McKay showed up unannounced on his office doorstep in the late afternoon of Tuesday, 5 December, with a man and woman who had somehow survived inhaling carbon monoxide fumes in their car in the nearby Eagle Hills. But after taking one look at the bedraggled couple and their wounds, he realized that they needed immediate medical attention and ordered the young constable to turn around and get them to St. Margaret's Hospital.

There, Dr. Brace carefully examined the gaping crevice in Rose's neck to determine the extent of the damage from the knife attack and then thoroughly cleaned and sutured her severed left sternomastoid muscle and stitched the skin back together. He also treated the back of her head. Fortunately, there was only a slight bruise from Ted's clumsy blows with the car crank. The cuts to her wrists, about two inches above the palm of each hand, were also superficial and were lightly dressed. Ted's wrist wounds, on the other hand, were much deeper—the subcutaneous tissue and tendons were exposed—and required several stitches to close.

Brace took detailed notes on the condition of the Bates, including their appearance and mental state. Ted was found to be "fairly intelligent, able to walk ... well nourished." But he still had not recovered from his ordeal in the car. "He has rather a dazed expression on his face," the doctor observed. Rose was equally traumatized. "Appeared in a nervous state," Brace recorded, "and shook as though she was very cold."[1] He also wondered whether she had been eating properly, for she appeared gaunt and lethargic. Little did he know that something inside was gnawing away at her.

Once the doctor had finished treating the pair, McLay took Ted to the local RCMP detachment, placed him in a cell, and instructed Archie Evanoff to keep an eye on him. At this point, the policeman wasn't sure if a crime had been committed, nor did he even know what had really happened. But he apparently feared that Ted might be suicidal and decided that it was best not to leave him alone.

McLay then hurried back to St. Margaret's to see Mrs. Bates, recuperating in bed in the women's ward. Although Dr. Brace was confident that the woman would likely survive her ordeal unless poisoning set in, the Mountie wanted to get a statement from her in the event that her condition deteriorated. He consequently asked the doctor whether he could speak to her and was told it would be okay.

McLay knew from his training at the RCMP academy that this interview could prove crucial down the road. He had to strike the right balance between getting at the truth and doing so in a way that any information could stand up in court, if it ever came to that. He decided to be extra careful. Even though no charges had been laid against Rose, McLay cautioned her that she did not have to say anything. But Rose wanted to talk about the incident, despite her weakened condition, and gave the young policeman a seven-page statement that he dutifully recorded in his notebook. She rambled on about where she was born, when she was married, when Jackie was born, how they started out in Glidden and went to Vancouver, and finally, how they had to go on relief and were shipped back to Saskatchewan.

The bulk of her statement was devoted to what had happened after they left Saskatoon in the borrowed car. Rose claimed that they were headed to Glidden to see if they could get the outstanding balance from the sale of the meat market, but that they got lost before having car trouble near the school. "We saw the car was not going to go," she explained to McLay, "so we pulled behind the driving shed and decided we would sleep in the car all night." That's when Jackie perished as they lay there in the back seat with the engine running to keep warm. "Jack, my boy coughed a little and then went to sleep," she explained. "Later he gave a jump. I asked him if he was cold and got no answer. I then found out he was dead. I lost my reason." Rose then described how they desperately tried to end their lives, how they sorely regretted not having a gun. But she adamantly maintained, "We had no intention of committing suicide when we left Saskatoon."[2] Jackie's death was entirely accidental and she was the one who begged her husband to end her life because of the loss of their son.

McLay read the statement back to Rose, added a sentence at the bottom to the effect that it had been given freely and voluntarily, and had her sign her name with his pencil. He then spoke to Dr. Brace, who doubled as the local coroner, about the need to retrieve the dead little boy from the back seat of the car in the schoolyard. Before leaving Biggar to perform their unpleasant task, McLay secured the services of a police matron to watch over Rose until his investigation of Jackie's death was further along. Something was not quite right. He could not understand, for example, why the couple was so intent on killing themselves after the death of their child.

McLay also hired a local man, Charles Mumby, to relieve Archie Evanoff from his guard duty so that the farmer could return home with him to Avalon late that afternoon. Getting the child was the policeman's first priority, but he was equally anxious to make a closer examination of the death car.

Back at the school, while a clutch of local people watched and waited nearby, Dr. Brace and Corporal McLay examined the stone-cold Jackie, checked his pockets for any notes, and then carried his rigid body to the back of the patrol car for transfer to the Biggar morgue. The policeman then inspected the motor and exhaust pipe and found that nothing had been tampered with. He also made a careful search of the car interior and found an assortment of items: a blood-stained butcher knife, razor blade, small hammer, several blood-soaked towels, a large and a small car crank, two small suitcases containing personal articles, and a woman's hat and purse. Perhaps the most poignant discovery were the two Big Little Books, *Mickey Mouse* and *Chester Gump*, that had slid out of Jackie's hands onto the back-seat floor as he fell asleep.

McLay wanted to leave the Bates' car where it had been found. After all, it might be a crime scene. But several local people warned him that parts could be stolen from it. He consequently towed the vehicle over to the Evanoff farmyard and then spent about another hour taking statements from Archie and Nick, the Horbenkos, and Jack Lee. McLay told Archie not to let anyone near the vehicle until he returned for it. He didn't have to worry. Anne Worobey, the second youngest of the Evanoff children, was thirteen at the time and later recalled how frightening it had been to have the pale and bug-eyed Ted and Rose Bates in their home that afternoon. The last thing she wanted to do during the night was to go outside to use the privy when the car in which the little boy had died was parked nearby.[3]

By the time McLay returned to the Biggar detachment early that evening, Corporal Charles Carey was waiting to speak to him about the investigation. All the corporal had heard was that a child had died under unusual circumstances and that the mother had to be hospitalized because her throat had been slashed by her husband. McLay gave a full accounting of what had transpired since he arrived at the Avalon school that afternoon and what he had been able to piece together about the incident. But he was still uncertain whether charges should be laid and for what crime. He had yet to take a statement from Ted and wanted to check his story against that of his wife.

In the days ahead, McLay and Carey would come to work closely together on the case. In fact, the chemistry between them made for an effective team. Born in Scotland and serving briefly as a policeman there, Donald McLay had tried his hand at farming in Ontario before enlisting in the force in September 1930. Upon completing his training at Regina, he spent his entire twenty-eight-year RCMP career with Saskatchewan's F Division. McLay's three sons would in time also become Mounties. Collectively, they and their father would have the distinction of over one hundred years of combined service. The sons were also the only three brothers from the same family in RCMP history to reach the rank of superintendent. But in December 1933, these accolades were for the future. The twenty-five-year-old McLay had still not investigated his first murder case.

Charles Carey, by contrast, was an older, more seasoned policeman. Born in England in 1895, he had served in the British Expeditionary Force during the Great War before immigrating to Saskatchewan to take up a soldier land grant near Eldersley. He too gave up farming to join the Saskatchewan Provincial Police in 1921 and then the RCMP seven years later when the provincial force was disbanded. By 1933, the thirty-eight-year-old corporal had over a dozen years' experience in several Saskatchewan communities under his belt and had handled all kinds of crimes, especially bootlegging. Carey's ability to get to the heart of a case nicely complemented McLay's natural investigative abilities.

Once McLay had apprised Carey of the situation, the pair set off for Wright's Funeral Home to meet Dr. Brace and to examine the dead child in the morgue. They could find no external marks of any violence—only bright red cheeks and large red blotches on the body—and would have to wait for the autopsy to confirm the exact cause of death. That was expected the next day. In the meantime, Brace said he would make preparations to hold a coroner's inquest as soon as possible.

The two policemen then headed to the hospital to talk to Rose Bates. Although McLay had already secured a statement that afternoon, Carey wanted to ask her a few questions to see whether she would tell the same story. Perhaps he was hoping her fatigue would be her undoing. But Rose repeated, almost verbatim, what she had said earlier.

That left Ted. Even though it was getting quite late, the Mounties returned to the detachment and roused their prisoner from his sleep. Carey took the lead, telling Bates that he was likely going to be charged with the attempted murder of his wife. In his defence, Ted offered a similar version of events, but he was not as convincing as Rose, probably because he was less certain and almost apologetic. It seemed as if the death of his son had been anything but an unfortunate accident, but actually part of a larger suicide pact.

The next morning, Wednesday, 6 December, Corporal Carey telephoned Crown prosecutor W. O. Smyth in Wilkie and discussed at length the questionable circumstances surrounding Jackie's death. Even though the police investigation was less than a day old, Carey recommended that both parents be charged with murder. Smyth agreed and instructed the Mountie to appear before the local justice of the peace, A. Davidson, and to secure arrest warrants. Dr. Brace also kept his pledge to move quickly on the matter. At 11:15 A.M., he opened a coroner's inquest at Wright's Funeral Home by swearing in six local men to the jury. Their first official act was to view the boy's lifeless body. The hearing was then adjourned for a week pending the receipt of the autopsy findings.

The case against the Bates was being put together quickly—maybe too quickly. The mounted police still had many leads to pursue as part of their investigation, both in Saskatchewan and Vancouver, and they had not managed to shake a confession from either Ted or Rose. But McLay and Carey were motivated by the fact that an innocent child had evidently died needlessly. What the parents were saying simply didn't add up, especially when a farmhouse was in plain sight directly across from the schoolyard, and the Evanoff family could have provided shelter from the cold weather. And what were they doing driving around the Eagle Hills, so far from the main highway?

No, there was more to this case than the fateful decision to sleep in a car overnight. It wasn't an accident. It was murder. And those on the front lines of the case were determined to hold the Bates accountable. They at least owed that to the dead boy.

Once Carey had secured the arrest warrants, he decided to drive with McLay to the Avalon school for the afternoon. He wanted to see first-hand where Jackie had died from the exhaust fumes and to go through McLay's notes from the moment he opened the car door and found the Bates inside. Carey was impressed with the constable's thoroughness. His only suggestion was that photographs of the site be taken sometime. The Mounties also made another search of the vehicle and discovered a second razor blade. McLay had found only one in the late afternoon darkness the day before and knew from Rose's statement that the couple had cut their wrists at roughly the same time.

Carey and McLay contemplated their next move over supper in a Biggar café. They were joined by Patrol Sergeant Williams from Rosetown, who decided to lend a possible hand to the investigation when he learned that the Bates were going to be arraigned for murder. Carey was convinced that the full story would come out by getting Ted or Rose away from their prepared script. It was just a matter of challenging them, taking issue with what was said in an effort to get one of them to say something incriminating. The obvious place to start was with Ted. After being found in the car, he was the one who told Jack Lee that his troubles were his alone, that he was mixed up. He was also the one who admitted to trying to kill Rose with his penknife, even turning over the weapon. If the police could play upon his confused state, while at the same time giving him a chance to get things off his chest, then maybe he would tell all. It was worth a try.

Back at the detachment, McLay brought Ted up from his downstairs cell, while Carey slipped outside to find a civilian to witness the interview—ironically, a butcher, Henry Dickey. Carey told Ted that the charge against him had been changed to murder and that he and Rose were about to be arraigned for causing the death of their son. He then asked the prisoner whether he had anything to say, after first warning him that he did not need to make a statement and cautioning him that any information he provided could be used against him in court.

Ted started to recount the same story that he and his wife had been telling for the past day, his constant repetition making it seem like the only story he knew. Carey reacted with disbelief, questioning whether what Ted was saying was actually true. The skepticism in the Mountie's voice left no doubt that he thought the prisoner was lying.

After a long pause, Ted admitted that he hadn't been truthful. With some urging from Carey, he said he was prepared to write down what had really happened. Bates prepared his statement at one of the Mounties' desks. It was remarkably brief, almost matter-of-fact. He seemed anxious to tell his story, anxious to get it out of his head and down on paper. Maybe he wanted to release himself from the heavy burden of what he and his wife had done. After all, this was a time when people were brought up to value honesty and knew the importance of telling the truth. Or perhaps he wanted forgiveness for murdering his only child. Whatever his reasons, Ted recounted in a few sentences what would become one of the most horrific incidents of the Great Depression.

Ted began his statement by talking about the bitter disappointment of being turned down for assistance in Vancouver and being shipped back to Saskatchewan as a relief case. "We understood that any place in Saskatchewan would do," he wrote. But when they got to Saskatoon, "they told us we had to go on to Glidden ... we did not want to go there." That's when they decided to commit suicide, taking the boy's life at the same time. In Ted's words, "we talked things over and decided to end it all."

"So we got a car," Ted explained, "and drove to the school yard and laid in the car with the idea of taking the gas from same." But it was only Jackie who died and "we were at our wit's end to know what to do." Rose wanted to die then and there, but Ted was too weak from the gas. "The Wife asked me to stab her in the heart but I could not manage that so I got the crank and tried to knock her insenseable but I had not the strength."[4] Finally, he slashed at Rose's neck with his penknife and then cut his wrists with a razor blade.

When Ted finished writing, he handed his statement to Carey, who asked him to sign it before he looked it over. The corporal and witness also added their own names. The police then showed Bates some of the items that had been taken from the car during their investigation, as well as the bloody penknife, and he readily identified them as the same items that he had mentioned in his statement. He also calmly demonstrated how he had used the car crank, striking at the air as if he were bashing Rose's head. To ascertain that the information had not been given under duress, Patrol Sergeant Williams made a point of asking Bates, in the presence of the civilian witness, how he had been treated by the two police investigators. Ted simply replied, "As a gentleman."[5]

Ted's statement corroborated what McLay and Carey had suspected since they first started to work together on the case—that the Bates, for some inexplicable reason, wanted to be poisoned by the carbon monoxide gas and that Jackie was an innocent victim of their scheme. In fact, when Ted's confession was lined up with the evidence and witness accounts that McLay had collected at Avalon, the police were well on their way to nailing the couple for the selfish murder of their son.

But they still hadn't got Rose to admit her role in Jackie's death, and without a confession, their case against her was weaker. Rose could blame everything on Ted and use her injuries to generate some sympathy. The two Mounties decided to confront Mrs. Bates with the confession they had just secured from her husband and left immediately for St. Margaret's Hospital. It was around 10 P.M. At the hospital, Carey and McLay asked to see Mrs. C. M. Kemp, the police matron who had been watching over Rose since her admission the day before. The pair wanted to know whether it was possible to speak to Rose. Kemp assured the two policemen that she was well enough to be interviewed and directed them to a private room on the second floor of the hospital while she retrieved the patient.

Rose entered the half-lit room, walking on her own, with the matron at her side. But the forty-one-year-old woman, her neck heavily bandaged, was still unsteady on her feet and would spend the next two weeks recuperating in hospital. She looked a shell of her former self in the shadowy light, something that a good wind would knock over.

Carey, as the senior Mountie, directed the interview. He began by asking Rose how she was feeling. She replied, "Fine," and then asked about her husband. Carey told her that he was okay, quickly adding that he had just given the police a formal statement. When Rose asked what Ted had said, the corporal dropped his bombshell, "He has told us everything." Rose didn't seem surprised by the news—she had always considered her husband to be weak—and responded, as if she had been waiting for this moment, "Well, I might as well tell you everything."

Corporal Carey helped Rose, now crying, to sit down before informing her that she and her husband had been charged with murder. "I know we'll hang," she blurted through tears, "and we both deserve it."[6] Carey stopped her from saying more with the warning that she did not need to speak to the police and that anything she said could be used as evidence at her trial. Like her husband an hour earlier, though, Rose was resigned to telling all.

Carey wanted Mrs. Bates to prepare her statement in her own hand, but when she said she did not feel strong enough, he suggested that it was probably too late to do much more. It might be best to get the matron to write it for her the next morning. Rose rejected the idea. She wanted to get it over with and agreed to dictate her statement to Constable McLay, while Carey and Mrs. Kemp served as witnesses. It took nearly half an hour to complete and then almost as much time to read aloud, as McLay slowly pointed to each word with his pencil while the matron looked on from his side. When he had finished, Rose nodded her head in agreement. McLay added a few lines to the effect that the statement was "given freely" and "all true" and read them over in the same manner. Everyone in the room then signed their name.

Rose's eight-page confession provided the detail that was missing in her husband's shorter account, but the two statements had one thing in common: Jackie had died because his parents had chosen suicide over going back to Glidden and facing the shame of being destitute. Her statement also squarely laid the blame for the tragedy on Ted. "My husband and I made a pact to end it all," Rose stated near the beginning, "meaning to end our lives and also the boy's, my son Jack. My husband suggested this. He even suggested that we get a car and drive out in the country and get poisoned with gas fumes ... My husband told me he knew that was an easy way to die."

Rose also spoke of how she stoically faced death in the back seat of the car with Ted and her son, the unwitting victim of their suicide plan. As she tried to fall asleep, she recalled, "I thought of everything, meaning, what I was doing ... I fully realized what I was doing and I prepared myself to meet the end." That end, however, befell only Jackie, and the rest of the statement told of the panic and horror that gripped the couple as they frantically tried to find a way to "finish it" with their young son lying lifeless between them.[7]

Mrs. Kemp would later report that Rose was "quite cheerful ... quite alert" when she gave her statement to the police.[8] Carey and McLay said much the same thing. Indeed, at the end of the interview, all were somewhat taken aback by how she talked so openly about the grisly incident. Most likely, it was Rose's way of coping, a way of pushing to the side the nightmare of having just killed her son. It certainly raised concerns about her mental fitness, something that would be questioned in the coming weeks and months.

One thing was clear, though. Rose was angry with Ted and went after him with ghoulish delight. She told them that he did not have the guts to cut his wrists deeply enough with the razor blade. She also remarked that the only reason she was still alive, sitting there in the hospital, was because her husband was "too yellow" to go through with it.9 But now that she had revealed what really happened in the schoolyard, she said, "I will sleep tonight now that I have told the truth and got it off my conscience."10

By the time McLay and Carey returned to the detachment, it was near midnight. But their day was far from over. Allan Bernbaum and his partner, Charles Allen, from the Allan Service Station in Saskatoon, were waiting there for them. McLay had informed the men earlier in the day that a grey Chevrolet coach, with a card in the front window bearing the company name, was part of a police investigation. Bernbaum explained how the Bates had come to the service station that past weekend looking to rent a car for a day and that they had driven off in the coach late Monday morning. "I have not seen any of these people since, nor have I seen the car since," he said in his statement. "Both the adults appeared normal in every way."11

Bernbaum and Allen wanted to take the car back to Saskatoon, but were told that it had to be examined first before being released. This inspection could have waited until the next day, but now that they had confessions from Ted and Rose, the mounted police were curious to see how easily the car exhaust could seep into the interior. McLay consequently drove to Avalon with the two men and towed the vehicle back to Biggar, returning around 2:30 A.M. Carey and Williams did the

1. RCMP Constable Donald McLay, the first policeman on the murder scene, was heralded for his handling of the Bates case. (Dave McLay)

2. The crumbling cement steps and foundation are all that remain of the Avalon school today. (Bill Waiser)

3. Corporal Charles Carey parked his patrol vehicle in the same position as the Bates car in the Avalon schoolyard as part of the RCMP investigation. (Saskatchewan Archives Board, R-A 7513)

4. A row of cars parked outside the new Glidden Community Hall. (*As It Happened: A History of the RM of Newcombe #260*)

5. This photograph of Glidden in the early 1920s was probably taken from the top of one of the grain elevators. (*As It Happened: A History of the RM of Newcombe #260*)

6. R. A. McDonald, proudly standing before his car, operated a dry goods business in Glidden in the booming 1920s. (*As It Happened: A History of the RM of Newcombe #260*)

7. Glidden Ladies Aid, 1925–26. The woman in the back row, third from the right, could be Rose Bates. *(As It Happened: A History of the RM of Newcombe #260)*

8. Glidden Ladies Community Club, 1926. The unidentified woman holding the baby in the middle row, second from the right, bears a striking resemblance to Rose Bates. *(As It Happened: A History of the RM of Newcombe #260)*

9. Jackie Bates attended Glidden Consolidated School (#2726). *(As It Happened: A History of the RM of Newcombe #260)*

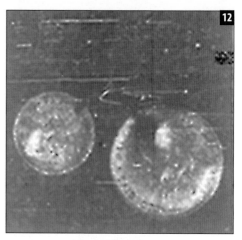

10. Children attending Jackie's funeral in the Glidden Community Hall. This newspaper photograph and others were scanned from microfilm copies of the newspapers. There are no surviving copies of the original photographs. (*Saskatoon Star-Phoenix*)

11. Young women attending church services at the Avalon school (#4077) in 1932. (*A Harvest of Memories: A History of Rural Wilkie*)

12. The two lucky coins, one British, the other Canadian, that Ted Bates kept over his bedroom door in Vancouver. (*Vancouver Sun*)

13. One of the Vancouver grocery stores (at Fifteenth Avenue and Kingsway) operated by Ted Bates in the fall of 1933. (*Vancouver Sun*)

14. Jackie's two Big Little Books: *Mickey Mouse, the Mail Pilot* and *Chester Gump at Silver Creek Ranch*. (Bill Waiser)

15. Jackie Bates (left) and his childhood friend Harry McDonald in Glidden in 1933. (Harry McDonald)

The only known portraits of the Bates family (Ted, Jackie, and Rose). (*Saskatoon Star-Phoenix*) The photographs first appeared in the *Saskatoon Star-Phoenix* only days after Jackie's death. It is not clear how the photographs were secured by the newspaper since the parents were in police custody at the time.

16. Corporal Charles Carey (performing as a clown in a Biggar theatre production) led the mounted police investigation. (Biggar Museum)

17. Saskatoon lawyer Harry Ludgate (shown here in his University of Saskatchewan graduation photograph) defended the Bates. (U of S Archives, B-180)

18. Biggar lawyer Walter O. Smyth served as Crown prosecutor in the Bates case. (Lu-Anne Demetrick)

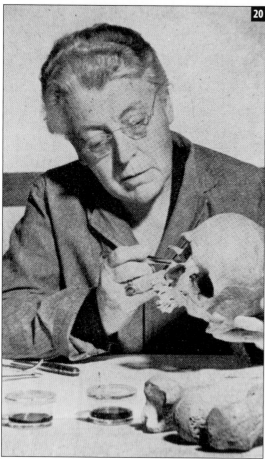

19. Both the coroner's inquest and preliminary hearing were held in Biggar in mid-December 1933. (Biggar Museum)

20. Dr. Frances McGill, Saskatchewan's provincial pathologist, attributed Jackie's death to carbon monoxide poisoning. (Saskatchewan Archives Board, R-A 12654)

21. Dr. W. D. Brace conducted the coroner's inquest into Jackie's death. (Biggar Museum)

inspection in the detachment garage. They found wide slots where the pedals passed through the floorboards, a wide crack where the floorboards came up to the dash, and two large holes in the car body underneath the rear seat. Any one of these openings, they concluded, would have allowed deadly fumes to flow into the interior, especially given how the car was parked.

Later that same day, now Thursday, Ted was arraigned for murder in the Biggar detachment. The preliminary hearing was set for the following Friday, 15 December. He was then taken to Wright's Funeral Home to make a formal identification of Jackie's body before the provincial pathologist performed the autopsy later that evening. By this time, two days after being discovered in the car in Avalon schoolyard, Ted appeared to have fully recovered from his brush with death from carbon monoxide poisoning. The only visible reminder of the incident was the bandages covering his slashed wrists.

What people still couldn't understand, though, was his complete lack of remorse over the loss of Jackie. He displayed no sign of emotion, even after he confessed that his son's death had been planned as part of his suicide pact with Rose. In fact, the man who had been initially hired to keep a suicide watch over Ted was amazed by how well he ate and slept in custody. Not even the sight of Jackie's body in the morgue moved him that morning. All Ted said was, "That is the body of my son." And that was it—no gasp, no tears, no other words. According to Constable McLay, who was with him, "He acted just as if he was identifying a shank of beef on his shelves."[12]

Rose behaved much the same way. Carey sent a police car to the hospital to take her to the funeral home, but she flatly refused to go. In fact, Rose never saw her little boy again after she was helped out of the car at the Avalon school. She might still have been in shock, her recovery slowed by the injuries she had sustained. Or maybe it was denial. Perhaps she didn't want to think about how she and her husband had killed their only child. It was much less painful to laugh and joke with the other patients and nurses in the ward. Mrs. Kemp, the police matron watching over her, considered her "hard-boiled and heartless."[13]

Rose saw Ted for about fifteen minutes Thursday afternoon before she was arraigned for murder in a special court session at St. Margaret's Hospital. It was the first time the pair had been together since Constable McLay had brought them to Biggar. The police apparently thought it would be best if Ted was at Rose's bedside during the proceedings. Justice of the Peace A. Davidson read the charge against her in the ward and then remanded her to the custody of the police matron. Rose listened stoically during the brief hearing and didn't start to cry until she was alone again with Mrs. Kemp.

The episode provided more fodder for the newspapers, which had been busy churning out lurid details about the incident since the story first broke. Much of what was initially reported was a melodramatic mixture of hearsay and speculation. The *Vancouver Sun*, for example, claimed that a berserk Ted, after being denied relief in Saskatoon, stabbed Jackie to death as they sat in a car, struck Rose with the car crank and stabbed her, and then cut his own throat.

These kinds of exaggerated reports were unavoidable given the sensational nature of the case. But within a few days, the newspapers began to carry remarkably accurate features based on leaked information coming out of Biggar. It seems that Corporal Carey had no qualms about talking to the press. Reporters had also done their own homework and found people willing to talk about the family's past in Saskatchewan and on the west coast. The *Saskatoon Star-Phoenix* even managed to secure photographs of the Bates from happier times.

Editorialists, meanwhile, seized upon the incident to blast the relief system. The *OBU Bulletin*, a radical labour newspaper, claimed that destitute Canadians had to choose between socialism or suicide. Bob Bouchette, in his "Lend Me Your Ears" column in the *Vancouver Sun*, called it "a social murder." "Young Jack Bates," he wrote in defence of Ted and Rose, "was slain in cold blood by society."[14]

The *Edmonton Journal* was more circumspect, suggesting that the tragedy could have been prevented if the administration of relief had been less humiliating and more compassionate. "It was all so unnecessary, all so pitifully futile," it commented. "These strangely doomed parents appear to have failed in life, to have failed in death."[15]

One of the angles pursued by the newspapers was the reaction to the tragedy in Glidden. No one in the village had heard from Ted and Rose since they had left for Vancouver the previous fall, except for Stan Elliot, who had been trying to collect the money from the sale of the meat market. Like thousands of other Saskatchewan families during the Depression, the Bates had moved on to try their luck elsewhere, and their few years in Glidden would normally have been forgotten over time. Now, it was being reported from Biggar that the Bates had balked at returning home as a relief case, to the point where they were apparently willing to take their lives and that of their son.

The news of Jackie's death, apparently at the hands of his parents, rocked the small community. It didn't seem possible, no matter how bleak or desperate life had become during the Depression. After all, others had faced similar predicaments at the time and found a way to survive. Why not the Bates? Why did they choose suicide when help was just a train ride away? And how could they plot the cold-blooded murder of the child they cherished?

It would have been perfectly understandable if their former friends and neighbours turned their backs on Ted and Rose in horror over what they had done. But the people of Glidden, the very people they had been too ashamed to face, refused to abandon the family in their time of need. Instead, the villagers saw the Bates as unfortunate victims of the Depression—a couple, once full of pride and hope, who had cracked under the strain and really did not know what they were doing. "Those of us who knew these people," reasoned merchant George Couper, "know that their minds had snapped ... they were weak and sought the easy way out."[16]

It's debatable, though, whether the motives of Couper and others who rallied around the family were entirely altruistic. Those who had helped establish Glidden had pinned their hopes for success on its great future, and they had to demonstrate that the village was a far better place than Ted and Rose had made it out to be. Otherwise, failure to do so would be an admission that they had made a bad choice in settling in Glidden. It was therefore in the interests of the village and its leaders to suggest that the Bates family had been destroyed by a flawed relief system.

The community moved quickly to deal with the fallout from the sordid incident. "Everybody's heart went out to them," recalled Jackie's childhood friend, Harry McDonald. "Maybe they didn't feel it but the town held hands out to them."[17] Harry's father was one of several local merchants who started to collect money for Jackie's funeral and for the legal defence of his parents. He also helped spread the word about a mass meeting that the village council called for Saturday to give people a chance to talk publicly about the tragedy.

The most urgent need was securing legal assistance, especially when the preliminary hearing for Ted and Rose was a little more than a week away. That task fell to their long-time friend Stan Elliot. The most obvious choice would have been either John Diefenbaker or Emmett Hall, a future prime minister and Supreme Court judge, respectively. Both had built their reputations on handling similar cases in Saskatchewan. Then, there was Hal Ebbels, a brilliant Saskatoon criminal defence attorney; he committed suicide a few years later, another victim of the Depression. Or Elliot could have asked Peter Makaroff, Canada's first Doukhobor lawyer, who later worked alongside Hall in defending those charged in the police-provoked 1935 Regina Riot.

But Elliot turned to Harry Ludgate, a Saskatoon lawyer whose practice revolved largely around police court work in the west-central part of the province. It's quite likely that as a justice of the peace Elliot would have known Ludgate personally and seen him in action. Contacted the same day as the arraignments, Ludgate readily agreed to defend the Bates on the informal understanding that his fees would be covered by the community. In fact, within hours of taking on the case, he informed the commander of the RCMP Saskatoon subdivision that he now represented the couple.

He also telephoned the Biggar detachment Thursday night and told Ted, who was fetched from his cell to take the long distance call, not to give any further statements to the police. Ludgate then called St. Margaret's to deliver the same message to Rose, only to learn from the police matron that she had already confessed to the murder of her son the night before. "That's too bad," he replied, "but perhaps we can work it out that she was too weak."[18] Mrs. Kemp knew where the lawyer was headed and responded that Rose's statement had not been given under duress, that she had actually waved away the suggestion that she wait until the next morning before telling the police what really happened. The call ended with Ludgate repeating his request that Rose be instructed not to speak any more about the incident.

Ludgate muzzled his new clients in order to prevent them from saying anything more that could be used against them in court. But there was nothing the Saskatoon barrister could do about the findings of the post-mortem performed on Jackie's body that same evening at Wright's Funeral Home.[19] While RCMP patrol sergeant Williams took notes, Dr. Frances McGill conducted her examination of the eight-year-old boy in the presence of the local undertaker, two other doctors, and another police constable. Both McLay and Carey stayed away. They had evidently formed an attachment to the dead child and did not want to attend the autopsy. As the father of two young girls, Carey probably found it particularly tough. In fact, he would lose his eldest daughter, Jean, four years later to a ruptured appendix. [20]

Dr. McGill found Jackie's body, measuring four feet, eight inches, to be well developed, even slightly chubby. There was no sign of any recent trauma or injury. The only scar was a vaccination mark on his right arm just below the shoulder. His skin was noticeably rosy pink except where his armbands and garters had left white marks above each elbow and below each knee. His lips were even redder, almost bright cherry in colour—a telltale sign of carbon monoxide poisoning. Carbon monoxide readily bonds with hemoglobin, thereby inhibiting the ability of blood to carry oxygen. In fact, blood saturated in carbon monoxide is even brighter, more vivid, than oxygenated blood. That's why Jackie's lips, full of blood vessels, were so red.

On opening the body cavity, McGill discovered the muscles to be deep red in colour. So too was the blood in the heart, the kidneys, and the brain. She could find no evidence of any clotting and was therefore able to rule out thromboembolism as a possible cause of death. All the major organs were normal except for the liver, which was enlarged and pale yellow. Such colouration is typically an indicator of starvation. The boy had evidently not been eating properly over the past few months, but living off his body fat, forcing his liver to work overtime.

All of the pathological evidence was consistent with carbon monoxide poisoning. There was really no other possible conclusion. But before submitting her official report, Dr. McGill wanted to conduct some tests on Jackie's blood in her Regina laboratory. She also removed the stomach and its contents for further analysis. The pathologist had detected no poison during her examination, but wanted to ensure that she did not miss something before she ruled it out.

Constable McLay also signed over to McGill the two knives, two razor blades, and one of the towels that he had found in the car or taken from the Bates. The items were to be tested for the presence of blood. The mounted police also wanted to know if the large butcher knife was new. If it had been purchased in Saskatoon, then it would strengthen their case that the Bates' actions were premeditated.

Once the autopsy had been completed, Dr. Brace released Jackie's body on Friday morning, 8 December, for burial. But who was going to look after the child's funeral arrangements? Certainly not the Bates.

Later that same day, Patrol Sergeant Williams escorted Ted by train to Saskatoon, where he was to be held in a mounted police cell until his preliminary hearing in Biggar the following week. As for Rose, she never took up the offer of a ride from the hospital to the funeral home to be with her dead son one last time. Instead, she sent Mrs. Kemp to see the boy and to tell her how he looked. Such callous behaviour would normally have shocked people. It was as if poor Jackie was being abandoned in death, as if he were some possession his parents no longer wanted or cared for. But as Williams observed in an internal police report after taking Ted to Saskatoon, "This case is very unusual, and has caused a lot of comment throughout the surrounding Districts, and a great deal of sympathy ... towards the Bates family."[21]

This sympathy was nowhere stronger than in Glidden. At an emergency meeting on Friday morning, the council endorsed Stan Elliot's hiring of Harry Ludgate to defend the beleaguered couple. It was also agreed that the village should assume responsibility for burying the Bates boy. These expenses were to be covered through voluntary donations to a Bates Trust Fund. Not only were members of the community to be called upon for contributions, but a special appeal was to be made to towns and villages along the local CN line and at places like Lemberg and Conquest where Ted had once lived and worked. The council was confident that it could raise the money, even though the village was carrying more than two thousand dollars on its books in uncollected taxes.

That clearly was the consensus the next day at an emotional mass meeting that had to be delayed a few hours to allow local farmers to get there over snow-covered roads. People from throughout the Newcombe Rural Municipality gathered in the community hall to hear what was being done to help the Bates in their time of need. The people in attendance first approved the establishment of a Bates defence fund. Immediately, a collection pail began to circulate through the hall. They then unanimously approved a resolution, to be sent to both the prime minister and Saskatchewan premier, blaming the tragedy on the Depression and the federal government's steadfast refusal to accept full responsibility for relief in the country. The Bates, according to the last part of the motion, had been placed in a kind of relief limbo: "Indigent persons applying for relief [should] be taken care of at the place where application is made and so avoid ... being placed in a position where they have to be moved long distances before they could secure relief with no certainty that relief would be granted when they reached their destination."[22]

What this sentence was effectively stating, albeit obliquely, was that the Bates family would have been no better off in Glidden. George Couper, the Glidden storekeeper in charge of the defence fund, said as much six weeks later in a letter imploring CN station agents to canvass their community for donations. "There is no relief here in Glidden for residents," he acknowledged, "so Bates could have been in as desperate shape had he returned here as he was in Vancouver except whatever charity he could receive at the hands of neighbours."[23]

Such an admission in the days after Jackie's death might have been seen as a justification for the Bates' actions—that they were right in not going back to Glidden. Rather than publicly acknowledge this, it was far better for the community to reach out to the Bates in their time of crisis and to offer whatever support it could muster. As the resolution charged, the Depression and the relief system may have triggered the incident in the Avalon schoolyard, but the more immediate concerns were burying the boy and then saving his parents from a murder conviction.

Eight-year-old Jackie was buried on Monday afternoon, 11 December. It had been exactly a week since he had left Saskatoon in the rented car, happily absorbed in his new Big Little Books in the back seat. The body had to be shipped by a circuitous route to Glidden for the funeral service. Since there was no direct rail link between Biggar and the village, the remains were sent first to Saskatoon and then back west along another CNR line to Kindersley. The final eighteen miles south to Glidden were by jigger, with the dead boy in his coffin tied down to the platform of the handcar.

Well over a hundred people attended the service in the community hall, including all of the kids from the local school who dutifully filed past Jackie's open coffin. Many still recoil today at the thought of seeing his body. Betty (Sawatzky) Reimer and her older brother Neil were both traumatized by the experience and have never forgotten it.[24] Nor has Harry McDonald, who was shocked when the school principal announced the death of his childhood friend, a friend he hadn't seen in over a year. "We marched around the coffin, an open casket," he recounted in his Vancouver home. "I can remember very distinctly to this day, Jackie Bates died of carbon monoxide poisoning and you could see it in his face."[25]

Other people who were children at the time have similar sad recollections. But it was probably Jean (Stannard) Hart, whose father ran the pool hall, who summed up the day best. When asked about the funeral, she candidly admitted, "Children were made to be mourners."[26]

Following the Glidden service, Jackie was buried on the extreme east side of the rural Madison cemetery. There was no graveyard in Glidden. The grave would be capped by a long convex cement slab with a bronze name marker that has since disappeared. Surviving records indicate that the funeral expenses came to sixty-five dollars, the exact amount in the defence fund.

Accounts of Jackie's funeral—the "victim" according to the headlines—made the front page in most western newspapers. Strangely, though, no mention was made in any of the articles that his parents were not there, only that they were awaiting trial for his murder.

Mrs. Kemp made a point of bringing a newspaper to the hospital the day after the funeral. She thought that Rose would want to hear about the Glidden service for her son and fought back tears as she read aloud the newspaper account at her bedside. All the patients in the ward started to cry as well, especially when they heard about Jackie's schoolmates shuffling by his coffin to say their goodbyes. Only Rose sat there stone-faced.

CHAPTER SIX

CERTAINLY
LOVED BY BOTH

J ackie Bates' funeral, according to the *Saskatoon Star-Phoenix*, was "the first chapter in one of the greatest tragedies ever to strike this district."[1] But how the sad story was going to play out was anybody's guess.

Biggar, a CN divisional point with about two thousand people at the time, was abuzz with gossip about the Bates case. And even though no one in town knew the couple or the personal circumstances behind their death pact, most were ready to blame the incident on the Depression. "I guess it was the hard times that caused it all," a man on the street explained to a visiting reporter.[2]

This kind of public sentiment, from the mounted police perspective, was like having one arm tied behind their back as they went about their investigation. At the very least, it made their work in preparing for the coroner's inquest and preliminary hearing all the more crucial. In sizing up the situation, Patrol Sergeant Williams of the Rosetown RCMP detachment readily admitted to his superiors that if the statements that the Bates had given to the police were ruled inadmissible, "then it will be a very difficult matter to prove the case."[3] Williams' pessimistic assessment was made only a few days after the Bates had been found in a gas-induced daze in the Avalon schoolyard. By the time Jackie had been buried, the police had gathered enough evidence to suggest that the death of the boy was premeditated and that his parents would likely have perished as well if they had bought more gas or pulled off the road sooner. Over the weekend of 9–10 December, RCMP detective/constable G. S. Nutt had secured a sworn statement from Allan Bernbaum at his Saskatoon gas station to the effect that Ted and Rose had lied about the reason for needing a car for the day. Nutt also interviewed Reverend Thomas Bunting and relief officer G. W. Parker and learned that the Bates family had been given temporary relief on the condition that they would be continuing on to Glidden by train, not looking to buy farm property north of the city, as they had told Bernbaum.

But where did the Bates get the money to rent the Chevrolet coach and to pay for a few precious gallons of gas, especially if they were broke? On a hunch, Nutt had the Saskatoon City Police check second-hand stores in the city, taking with them a description of the family. It was not long before they located a shopkeeper on the west side who had bought a robe from Rose. Her rings would turn up after a little more searching.

Another mounted policeman, meanwhile, had followed up on a call from J. T. Keyser of the Union Baggage Transfer office and discovered that the Bates had shipped three trunks to Vancouver prior to leaving Saskatoon on their fateful journey. This information in itself was potentially damning, but even more so, the police believed, if one of the trunks was found to contain a suicide note. Clearly, the investigation had to be expanded to include Vancouver.

Back in Biggar, Corporal Carey, after receiving the internal reports from Saskatoon, decided to have a chat with Mrs. Bates at St. Margaret's Hospital late Monday morning, even though her lawyer had expressly forbidden such conversations. He really had no business slipping behind counsel's back to interview Rose, but the policeman wanted to find out if she would help fill in some of the remaining pieces in the investigation puzzle.

Rose, still resting in hospital, was happy to see the Mountie. She had just spent a frustrating hour with Dr. Brace, the coroner, who claimed that he was collecting her medical history for his file. Rose suspected that the doctor was actually conducting a mental examination and complained to Carey, "I am not insane, I knew perfectly well what I was doing all the time, and I don't want anyone to think I'm crazy."

The corporal wanted to know if he could talk to her about the case. Rose said yes, adding that she was tired of being told to keep quiet. "I have done wrong, and I'm willing to be punished for it," she hissed, "and I do not see why the people of Glidden should interfere, and I do not want a lawyer."

Carey used the opening to see how much she was willing to tell, how far she was willing to go. He started by asking about Vancouver and what had happened there. Rose reported that they were down to their last thirty-five cents by the time Ted finally agreed to apply to the city for assistance. After being turned down, a stunned Ted evidently headed to city police headquarters and warned them, "I have been refused relief, what do you expect me to do, go home and slaughter my wife and child and then do myself in?"

Rose then recounted the ordeal of being sent back to Saskatchewan, even though they had no intention of ever returning to Glidden. That's when the pair decided on the suicide pact. She assured Carey that Jackie had no idea of where they were going or what they intended to do when they slipped away from Saskatoon in the rented car that fateful day. He was happily reading his new books in the back seat. She also stopped short of blaming her husband for all of their troubles. She would only concede that he was selfish and had wasted money in the past. This selfishness, Rose intimated, even extended to their suicide plan. She was the one, she candidly admitted, who suggested that they should end their lives—"the death pact met with his approval." But Ted wanted her and the boy to pass out first and then he would follow.[4]

Corporal Carey probably left St. Margaret's with a better appreciation of what he was dealing with. Whether he was more sympathetic towards the Bates was another matter. At this point in the investigation, his only focus was to try to find out as much as he could about their motives in order to help prove that Jackie's death was anything but accidental. That's why the Mountie had headed to the hospital to see what he could get out of Rose.

It's also why Carey drove to the Avalon school that afternoon with Biggar photographer Walter Randall to take pictures of the buildings and yard. In several of the photographs, Carey's police vehicle was parked in exactly the same place as the death car. With Randall's assistance, he also took measurements for a scale plan of the grounds.

Several local people were curious about Carey's activities and wandered over to the school to tell their stories about the incident and to ask about the Bates. It was during one of these conversations that the policeman discovered that a group of men had seen the grey coach parked next to the stable in the early evening of 4 December—without the engine running. It was only after they had shouted a few times that someone started the car. This was not trivial information. The Bates had initially claimed that they were lost that night, that they didn't know where to turn for help, and consequently kept the vehicle running to stay warm. From what the local farmers said, though, it appeared that the Bates did not want to be found and that they had another reason for being in the isolated schoolyard.

Carey returned to Biggar in the early evening to find a message from the commander of the RCMP Saskatoon office. Somehow, the Bates' lawyer, Harry Ludgate, had been alerted that Rose had been questioned again, and he did not like it. Carey was instructed not to take any more statements from the accused. The veteran policeman should have known better. By acting like a lone cowboy, he was jeopardizing the investigation by making it appear that undue pressure was being brought upon the accused. This was no ordinary criminal, but a mother, who had just lost her only child, recuperating in hospital from wounds inflicted by her husband. Ludgate could not have asked for a better weapon to attack the police handling of the case if it ever went to trial.

Carey took the warning in stride and focused his energies on getting ready for the inquest and preliminary hearing. He carefully went over the details of the case with Smyth, who had been handed the job of representing the Crown, and Constable Donald McLay from Rosetown. One of their most pressing duties was assembling a list of witnesses to be summoned.

There was also new evidence to digest. Sent to Glidden to look into the Bates' past, Constable William Lambert of the Kindersley RCMP detachment was shown a letter by Stan Elliott, the local justice of the peace. It was the note that Ted had posted from Perdue, just hours before the family pulled into the Avalon schoolyard. One simple sentence seemed to say it all: "We was coming back to Glidden but changed our minds."[5]

Saskatchewan premier J. T. M. Anderson also indirectly helped the prosecution when he issued a press release in which he adamantly maintained that the Saskatoon relief office was completely blameless in the tragedy. Anderson noted that the Bates had been provided with a room and meals during their weekend layover in the city—not "refused relief," as some newspapers had wrongly reported—and that the vouchers had been redeemed.[6] This assistance had been given in the expectation that they would take the Monday-morning train to Glidden. What more, Anderson implied, could the relief office have done under the circumstances?

It was a good question, one of many surrounding the gruesome incident. The other uncertainty was Rose Bates. What was she going to say if she were called upon to testify? She could be something of a wild card in the case.

The day after Carey had spoken to her at the hospital, Harry

Ludgate showed up in Biggar, ostensibly to talk to Rose about the inquest and hearing, but more likely to caution her that she wasn't helping things by talking so freely to the police. It was the first time lawyer and client had met face-to-face. During their interview over a pot of tea, Ludgate asked Rose what the police had said to her before she gave her statement. She responded, "Well, the usual thing." A curious Ludgate pushed for the exact words the Mounties had used. She replied that she had been told that "she might as well tell everything, that it would be better for her and better for them." Ludgate immediately wheeled around to Mrs. Kemp, the police matron, who was hovering nearby, and asked whether she would swear to that. She said no, that she had heard no such thing.

After Ludgate left, Kemp reminded Rose that she should be careful about what she said regarding the boy's death in her presence. Rose didn't care. She shot back that she intended to "tell the whole truth, the same as she had already told the police."[7]

Rose would get her chance when the coroner's inquest into Jackie's death opened at 2 P.M. on Thursday, 14 December. It had originally been scheduled earlier in the week, but had been moved to the day before the preliminary hearing to save money. Witnesses expected to appear before both proceedings would not have to wait around in Biggar at government expense. The change in date left the coroner scrambling to find a suitable venue since the Biggar town hall was already booked that day. He eventually secured Miller's Hall for five dollars, the most that the Saskatchewan Attorney General's department was willing to pay. It didn't seem to matter that the hall, normally used by the local Masons, was decorated with banners and other lodge symbols.

Arrangements also had to be made for an interpreter since some of the witnesses from the Avalon district were more comfortable speaking Russian. That role was filled by RCMP special constable Mervyn Black, who had been recruited as a secret agent but now held a desk job in

Saskatoon handling informants. Black arrived on the same morning train as prisoner Ted Bates, who had spent the past week in a Saskatoon police cell. During the trip, Reverend Lephson of the Christian Missionary Society recognized Ted from the newspaper stories and handed him a copy of the Gospel of St. John. It's not clear whether Ted appreciated the gesture or whether he was even looking for salvation after having spent several days mulling over what he and Rose had done.

Dr. Brace solemnly opened the inquest by calling out the names of the six jurymen: W. Brownlee (foreman), J. S. Bell, J. Miller, W. Keefe, C. E. Bick, and J. Mooney. All were drawn from the community and included, in order, a saddler, insurance agent, tobacconist, CN brakeman, druggist, and hardware merchant. Brace reminded them that they were still sworn from when they first met to view the dead boy's body at Wright's funeral home.

Walter Oswald Smyth, a thirty-three-year-old lawyer from nearby Wilkie, represented the Crown.[8] Slim in build with dark hair, blue eyes, and a moustache, the Montreal-born Smyth came from a legal family. His father had been a judge in Swift Current and he followed him into the profession after graduation from Whitmore Hall in Regina. His first practice in Kincaid was driven under by drought and the Depression, and he was forced to start over again in Wilkie in 1932, the same year the Bates had fled to Vancouver.

Although a small-town lawyer for much of his life, Smyth could tangle with the best from the big city. It was probably his Conservative connections, however, that secured him work as a prosecutor. This patronage was certainly needed. Like many other lawyers in the 1930s, he was often paid in chickens, cream, or whatever people had to offer for his legal advice. Smyth had a strong sense of community service that would later include a stint as mayor of Wilkie. He also liked to golf, curl, and play bridge, and often punctuated an amusing story with a deep belly laugh.

His opponent, representing the Bates, was the forty-four-year-old, balding, slightly stocky Henry Ludgate, or Harry as he was popularly known.9 Born in County Down, Ireland, Ludgate immigrated to Saskatoon in 1910, working first as a banker and then as a clerk at the courthouse. In May 1918, he was conscripted to serve in the Canadian Expeditionary Force, but was given his discharge so that he could enlist in the Royal Flying Corps. He never saw action. After the war, Second Lieutenant Ludgate studied law at the University of Saskatchewan. The names of his eleven-member graduating class in 1922 read today like a who's who of the Saskatchewan legal community and included four future judges. Then, there was Ludgate. If the poor grades on his university transcript are any indication, he barely scraped through. His heavy drinking was the obvious reason. It is usually the first thing that fellow lawyers recall about him today, almost as if it were "an occupational hazard" in his case.10 Later in Harry's life, when the booze had exacted its toll, J. M. Goldenberg and several other former classmates started a fund for his maintenance.

Ludgate carved out a career, if not a living, in the police courts. It was no coincidence that many of his clients were bootleggers who had run afoul of the provincial liquor act. At the time, beer and spirits could be purchased only in a government liquor store. This work made him a popular friend of both the local police and petty criminals and he often shared a drink with them.

In hiring Ludgate to defend the Bates, the village of Glidden got a decent lawyer. He knew his way around a courtroom and rarely missed much. He could also be something of a performer and used his Irish brogue and blackthorn walking stick to good dramatic effect. His real strength, though, was his word. If Ludgate said he was going to do something, he did it. And that's the best the Bates could ask for.

The first witness at the inquest was Saskatoon relief officer John J. McGrath. Under questioning by Smyth, he testified that Ted Bates had simply appeared at his office on the afternoon of Friday, 1 December, and asked for meals and accommodation for his family. Once it had been ascertained that the Bates had tickets to Glidden on the Monday-morning train, McGrath issued vouchers for the weekend. Ludgate posed no questions.

Next came Allan Bernbaum, who explained that the Bates were complete strangers, but that he had agreed to rent them his car so that they could check out some farmland north of Saskatoon. Smyth was particularly interested in how much gas was in the vehicle. Bernbaum said that there were only about two gallons in the tank and the Bates had paid for another six. He also reported that the gas tank was completely empty when he and his partner took possession of the car in Biggar after it had been inspected by the police.

Ludgate wanted to know about the running condition of the car and how, in Bernbaum's opinion as a mechanic, the exhaust might find its way inside. In response, the garage man claimed that his vehicle, although in good shape, was not airtight and that it would be possible for fumes to seep inside through the front floorboards. He also suggested, speaking hypothetically, that carbon monoxide could become trapped inside if a car were parked in a snowbank.

Bernbaum was about to return to his seat when Smyth asked him whether the man and woman who called at his service station were in the courtroom. The mechanic said yes and pointed to Ted and Rose. Smyth was lucky. Forgetting to get the identification into evidence was a serious oversight and could have been costly in a trial.

Corporal Carey was called to the stand next. Smyth started by asking the Mountie to compare Highway 14 between Saskatoon and Biggar with the rough road that ran north through the Eagle Hills to the Avalon school. The prosecutor mused, "And would it be possible in your opinion for a person to mistake highway no. 14 with this road?"

"Absolutely impossible," Carey answered.[11]

Smyth then led Carey through a detailed description of the school grounds and the buildings, often referring to the scale map that the corporal had prepared and the photographs taken by Randall at the crime scene. The pair spent considerable time discussing how the stable was difficult to see from the road and how the average car was too wide to fit through its doors. Carey concluded his testimony by presenting Smyth with a CN bill of lading. It showed that Ted had shipped three trunks collect to Vancouver the day he left Saskatoon in the rented car. Smyth entered it as an exhibit.

Stan Elliot, the Glidden justice of the peace and drayman, provided further damaging evidence: several letters penned by Ted. Three had been sent from Vancouver that fall and seemed to be the work of a desperate man on a downward spiral, failing in business and in life. Smyth read each of them into the record over Ludgate's objection. Elliot then handed over the letter that Ted had written in Saskatoon on Western Hotel stationery and later mailed from Perdue the day of the tragedy. Once again, Ludgate was on his feet in protest, but the coroner gave Smyth permission to read the letter to the jury and to enter it as an exhibit.

Smyth then asked whether Elliot had ever read in the newspaper about an incident a few years earlier in which a car got stuck in a snowbank north of Regina and the occupants had perished from carbon monoxide poisoning. This question seemed to take Ludgate by surprise and he muttered something about the matter being irrelevant to the inquest. But Smyth persisted. Elliot testified that the story was well known in the district and that the Bates were still living in Glidden at the time. Ludgate interrupted again and asked that his objection be noted in the record.

Ludgate had only a few questions for Elliot. After establishing that the drayman knew the Bates family "very well," he asked about Jackie's general health. Elliot responded, "Well, the only thing I would say, he was pale." The defence lawyer then wanted to know how the boy was looked upon by his parents. "He was certainly loved by both," Elliot affirmed.

Ludgate repeated the words aloud, so that their full force was felt in the courtroom: "The answer was 'he was certainly loved by both'." Smyth didn't want Elliot's testimony to end on that note and so he got him to admit that he knew little about the family after they left Glidden.

John Lee, the farmer who lived north of the Avalon school, was next in the procession of witnesses. He recounted how the Bates had pulled into his yard around suppertime on 4 December, wanting to buy some gas for their car. He further testified that he had given them about a gallon and then invited the family inside for a meal before seeing them off roughly an hour later, headed south towards Highway 14. Smyth was curious as to whether there had been any talk around the supper table about the Bates becoming stranded in the hills and being forced to spend the night in the car. Lee reported that Rose had brought the matter up and that he had flatly told her that it was "a silly idea because of the gas from the engine."

Thomas Hull, the next witness and a guest at Lee's home that same evening, provided similar testimony. When asked by Smyth—not once, but twice—whether the Bates had been warned about the danger of sleeping in the car with the engine running, he said yes both times. Ludgate tried to counter these statements by getting both farmers to remember how cold it was and whether the Bates had complained about being chilled when they stepped inside for supper. He seemed to be implying that the Bates might have had a good reason for finding a way to keep warm.

Smyth then directed the inquiry to what had happened in the Avalon schoolyard the night of Jackie's death. Archie Evanoff, whose farmhouse was across the road from the school, began to testify about the strange car he had spotted from his kitchen window. But by the third question, a frustrated Smyth asked RCMP interpreter Mervyn Black to step in and translate for the witness. For almost an hour, working through Black, the prosecutor posed over fifty questions about the erratic behaviour of the driver of the mystery car. Ludgate eventually interjected—not necessarily to complain about the slow pace, but rather about the way in which the questions were being asked. Smyth was phrasing them so that Evanoff could provide simple, at times one-word, answers. "My learned friend," Ludgate sarcastically remarked, "might just as well give evidence himself." Smyth ploughed ahead, promising to be finished with the witness soon. Ludgate was reduced to grumbling, "Now, now," whenever a leading question was asked.

Evanoff was followed on the stand by Peter and Nellie Horbenko, who had found the Bates in their car the next morning, then his son, Nick Evanoff, and finally another neighbour, Mrs. Mark Nikitin.

Smyth's plodding style of questioning quickly got under Ludgate's skin. He erupted at one point to declare that much of the testimony that the prosecutor seemed so intent on eliciting had no bearing on the issue at hand. "I submit that the jury could listen to this for the next four years," an exasperated Ludgate declared. The coroner ruled that Smyth's questions were for the benefit of the jury, but Dr. Brace did gently encourage him to try to restrict his examination of the witnesses to the circumstances behind the child's death.

Ludgate didn't intervene again. When it came his turn to ask questions, he sought only greater detail or precision, such as the exact time when certain events were said to have happened. There was nothing to be gained at this stage in challenging the witnesses. He was more interested in learning what he was up against in defending his clients.

By late afternoon, nearly four hours into the inquest, a subdued mood had settled over the courtroom. The death of a young child was depressing business, and it weighed heavily on the proceedings. Suddenly Smyth created a minor stir by requesting that Rose Bates be called. Ludgate, barely out of his chair, strenuously objected, insisting that neither she nor Ted should be forced to give evidence regarding the death of their son. Dr. Brace listened to the lawyers' arguments before grasping at a compromise offered by Ludgate: that the couple only be asked questions about the identification of the dead boy's body.

Up to then, Ted had sat passively next to his wife and a police matron as the tragic details of his family's last few days together became part of the court record. The only time he showed any emotion was when Rose wept at the more poignant parts of the testimony, and he tried to comfort her. For many in the courtroom that day, the Bates appeared to be a loving couple, caught up in a terrible tragedy because of the Depression.

Rose, with her throat still bandaged from the knife wounds, was questioned first. Smyth asked her whether the body found in the car in the Avalon school was that of her child. "He was," she answered.

"When did you next see the body of the boy?" the prosecutor continued.

"I didn't see him after I left," Rose frowned.

"What was the name of the boy?"

"Jack Edward."

Smyth then turned to the coroner and wanted to know if he was right in thinking that he could ask no other questions. "That's my ruling," Dr. Brace confirmed.

Ted went next. Smyth began a long-winded preamble that prompted Ludgate to shout, "Oh, just put the questions." Stung by the outburst, the prosecutor asked a series of questions that established that the boy in the car was Jack Edward Bates and that Ted had later identified the body at the Biggar morgue. Ludgate then popped up and slipped in the question, "Had your son been subject to fainting spells?" Ted quickly said yes.

Smyth, still walking back to his seat, swung around in protest, declaring that evidence from the witness was supposed to be limited to the identification of the body. "I think Mr. Ludgate overstepped the mark a little," the coroner observed, but he issued no directive to the court recorder to remove the question and answer from the transcript.

It seemed like a good time for a supper break so Brace adjourned the proceedings until 8 P.M. When court reopened, Constable Donald McLay of the Rosetown RCMP detachment took the stand. Neither Ted nor Rose was there to listen to his testimony.

Since McLay had been the first policeman to appear at the scene of the crime, Smyth tried to pump him for as much information as possible. He began by asking the Mountie about the position of the car and what had happened when he looked inside. McLay described how he had found a man and a woman sitting in the back seat with a seemingly lifeless little boy between them. "The woman, Mrs. Bates," he recounted, "said her son had died of poison from the car and she had asked her husband to do her in ..."

"I object to this evidence," Ludgate thundered. "We are only concerned here with the boy, nothing else. It is irrelevant." Smyth asked the coroner for a ruling. Brace agreed to record Ludgate's objection, but didn't think the testimony was irrelevant.

McLay continued to report what Rose had said and then explained how he had taken the injured couple first to the Evanoff farmhouse and then to Biggar for treatment. He also provided a list of the items from the car. These included the heavy crank that Ted had tried to knock Rose out with and the two books that Jackie had apparently been reading. All three items were entered as exhibits.

Ludgate objected again when Smyth asked about the statement that Ted had provided to the police while being held in the Biggar detachment. He also objected to any questions about his client's physical condition at the time. Dr. Brace didn't share these concerns and allowed the information to be admitted. But Smyth wasn't satisfied and wanted to know why Ludgate kept interrupting. The defence counsel snapped, "Any time a statement is made there are always objections to it. Don't you know that?"

McLay wasn't fazed by the wrangling between the two lawyers and forged ahead with his testimony. He described the circumstances behind Ted's written confession and then, over Ludgate's objection, read it aloud to the jury before it was tendered as an exhibit. He also read into the record the two statements that Rose had provided at the hospital, but not before defence counsel registered his protest.

Ludgate began his cross-examination by innocently asking McLay how long he had been on the force. When the constable replied, "About four years," Ludgate sprung the trap and suggested that it was probably the mounted policeman's first case of any importance. There followed a rapid-fire exchange between the two, as Ludgate peppered the young Mountie with question after question in a thinly veiled effort to confuse him or at least get him to contradict himself. But McLay, who was the only witness that evening, held his ground.

Ludgate couldn't understand why the police, on the one hand, were worried about Rose's condition and yet, on the other, believed she was well enough to give an official statement. "Was she feeling lively as a cricket?" Ludgate queried.

"Well, she wasn't feeling ill ... as a matter of fact she smiled quite a few times," McLay responded.

"Was her condition alright?"

"She was alright."

"As far as you care?"

"No Sir!"

Ludgate also wanted to know exactly how many times the police had interviewed Rose and why some of McLay's own testimony that evening seemed to go against what she had said in her statements. "Would you like to pick out certain parts for us to believe?" he sarcastically quipped at one point. The defence lawyer then turned to the matter of how Rose had been cautioned by the police, repeating what she had told him in hospital earlier that week.

These remarks brought Smyth into the fray. "Is my learned friend giving evidence?"

"Please be quiet," Ludgate growled.

"Pardon me," the prosecutor persisted, "I am asking if my learned friend is disclosing the confidence ... is he giving evidence or what?"

"I don't know that he should," chimed in the coroner.

Ludgate argued that it was a fair question, but then shifted his focus to whether or not Rose was really aware of what she was being asked to provide, given that her son had just perished. "She appeared quite sane to me," McLay maintained. "She had a wonderful recollection of everything that took place." Ludgate concluded with a few questions about Jackie's health. The constable reported that the boy apparently had been subject to fainting spells. When Ludgate asked for clarification, McLay said that Rose claimed that the boy had nearly fainted at the Allan Service Station before leaving Saskatoon on their fateful trip. "That would be the same day," Ludgate observed. "Oh, well, that's all."

With McLay's grilling over, the coroner adjourned the hearing until 9 A.M. the following morning. Although it was only an inquest, the Rosetown Mountie had delivered devastating evidence against the Bates. Indeed, many of the local papers were hailing him as the Crown's star witness after his spirited performance under fire. The RCMP commissioner even issued a letter of commendation.

When the inquest reconvened Friday morning, Smyth recalled Corporal Carey to the stand in order to ask him about the reliability of the testimony provided by McLay the night before. Carey said he could "corroborate in detail" McLay's version of events except for the first few hours of the investigation when he was away dealing with another matter. RCMP patrol sergeant Williams then took the stand briefly to report on his examination of the Bates' car. He testified that exhaust fumes could easily have entered the vehicle through the floorboards. Ludgate picked up on this information and wanted to know whether the car could have been in that condition for some time. "I suppose so," answered Williams.

The two Mounties served as a kind of warm-up act to the real headliner that morning, Dr. Frances McGill, the provincial pathologist.

Born in Manitoba, the fifty-six-year-old McGill had lost both parents after they drank contaminated water at the 1900 Brandon Fair. That experience probably influenced her decision to give up her career as a rural schoolteacher and to train as a doctor at the University of Manitoba. Upon graduation, McGill interned at the Winnipeg provincial laboratory where she developed her lifelong interest in pathology. In 1918, she moved to Regina to assume her new position as provincial bacteriologist for Saskatchewan—just in time to deal with the deadly Spanish flu epidemic. She was also responsible for the treatment of venereal disease, especially among returning Great War soldiers. Her office and lab were housed on the top floor of the Legislative Building, while the animal cages had to be kept on the roof.

Four years later, in 1922, McGill was running things as director of Saskatchewan laboratories and provincial pathologist—the first woman in Canada to hold such a position. But she found her real calling the following year when she began to assist the RCMP in their criminal investigations. McGill's forensic work for the police took her to all parts of the province to deal with puzzling and at times bizarre deaths. Sometimes the circumstances were nothing short of distasteful, especially if the body had not been found before decomposition had set in. But she invariably came up with an explanation that made sense of the crime scene. If the case were particularly intriguing or unusual, she gave it a name, such as the Deserted Shack Murder, the Bran Muffin Case, or the Straw Stack Murders.

The police who worked alongside the pathologist marvelled at her seemingly tireless energy and her willingness to put aside her own work to help them whenever and wherever her services were needed. The day she performed the autopsy on Jackie Bates' body, for example, she travelled from Regina to Saskatoon by train the night before, by police car to and from Biggar, and then back to Regina on an overnight sleeper. This kind of dedication made McGill popular with the force and she was affectionately known as "Doc." She also became a regular fixture at preliminary hearings, coroners' inquests, and trials, where she dispensed her forensic findings in a no-nonsense fashion.

McGill had no patience for lawyers' antics and could thrust and parry with the best of them. One time during a murder trial, her report that the stains inside a man's pocket were human blood came under intense scrutiny. The defence attorney wondered how she could presume to be an expert on the contents of men's pockets. "Not at all," she tartly replied. "I am not a member of the legal profession." McGill also grew annoyed when questioned why she had never married. She regarded it as sheer folly for a woman to abandon a promising career for a man. Besides, she was happy with the company of her small circle of friends and loved to cook for them and to play bridge. And whenever she got the chance, she would go riding for hours outside Regina on her horse.

Dr. McGill's official, three-page report on the death of Jackie Bates was released just before the inquest, and Walter Smyth wanted first to go over it with the pathologist for the benefit of the jury. She explained that the body's rosy pink colour was indicative of carbon monoxide poisoning. "The body suggested that," she asserted, "as soon as I saw it." McGill then described what she found when she performed the autopsy—how the boy's cherry red blood and bright pinkish organs were "all positive, markedly so" for carbon monoxide gas. There was no other possible explanation for his death, she pronounced with an air of certainty. Fainting spells had nothing to do with it.

But why, Smyth asked, did Jackie perish when both his mother and father were in the back seat of the car with him, inhaling the same fumes from the exhaust? McGill responded that the child's larger lungs in proportion to his body meant that his blood and organs were more quickly saturated with carbon monoxide than those of his parents. Smyth could have ended his examination of the pathologist at that point. He had got what he wanted from the doctor, and the autopsy report had been entered as an exhibit. But for some inexplicable reason, he decided to explore the after-effects of carbon monoxide poisoning.

McGill seemed initially reticent to answer his questions. Was "dulled mentality," he speculated, a frequent occurrence? "It happens," she agreed.

"Loss of memory?"

"I don't know."

Smyth also mused about how long the effects could last and got the doctor to comment that it could take days, if not longer. "There are cases where they have never recovered," McGill offered.

Smyth suddenly realized what he was doing—calling into question the reliability of the Bates' statements—and he requested a brief adjournment. The break, however, only gave Harry Ludgate more time to consider how he was going to exploit Smyth's mistake and he pounced as soon as court resumed. He raised the hypothetical example of "unnamed parties" being in an accident, just like the Bates, and asked the doctor whether it would be possible to accurately determine their mental state through casual conversation. McGill confessed it would be "pretty hard."

Smyth tried to undo the damage by immediately recalling Corporal Carey. He was anxious to have him testify about the behaviour of the Bates after they were removed from the car and brought to Biggar. He first asked about Rose. Carey stated that she appeared lucid and had "a very clear recollection" of what had happened. So too did Ted. The corporal joked that he had recovered so quickly from his ordeal that "every meal was cleaned up. He left nothing on the plate ... it would be rather expensive [to feed him] I think."

Ludgate shared the laugh before demanding to know exactly how Carey had decided that the couple was fine. "Not hesitating in anything said," he answered, "the flow of speech quite natural." But didn't patients at the Battleford asylum, Ludgate retorted, talk glibly at times? "They do, yes," a sheepish Carey conceded.

Ludgate, sensing that he had the Mountie on the ropes, didn't let up. "Do you consider Mrs. Bates acted normally for a woman who loved her boy?"

"It struck me," the policeman observed, "that she has not shown apparent signs of grief."

"Not natural is it?"

"Not for a mother, no."

Smyth frantically scanned the courtroom to find a rebuttal witness. In desperation, he turned to John Lee, the Avalon-area farmer who had fed the family the night of the tragedy. When asked how Ted had acted around the supper table, Lee hesitated and had trouble giving a definitive answer. Maybe it was because the farmer couldn't get out of his mind the memory of Constable McLay taking the couple to the Evanoff home to warm up after their night in the car.

Ludgate sensed that something still troubled Lee and suggested, "You were not very normal yourself?"

"Well," he paused before sighing heavily, "the next day when I saw them, no, I was upset a lot. I will admit that, sure."

Lee was the last inquest witness. It seemed that there was nothing more to say or to be gained by going over details of the sad case. The six jurymen evidently agreed. When Dr. Brace asked whether any of them had any questions, they just shook their heads.

Smyth, at this point, asked the coroner to instruct the jury that in deciding its verdict it should assign blame for the death of Jackie. Ludgate chose not to argue the matter, but put forward his own request: that the jury consider asking for a mental examination of the two accused. Brace chose to ignore the advice and sent the jury off at 10:15 A.M. to consider simply when, where, and how the boy died. They were back in just fifteen minutes with a verdict that really didn't settle the question: Jackie Bates had died of carbon monoxide poisoning "while in a car in charge of his father and mother."

Ted and Rose barely had time to digest the decision before their preliminary hearing got underway in the same courtroom only forty-five minutes later. In fact, it seemed as if it was their fate—some might argue, their punishment—to go through the same ordeal again, only this time to determine whether they should proceed to trial on a murder charge. The only difference was that Police Magistrate Joseph T. Leger was now in charge and that he would be deciding their fate, not a jury.

Leger, a New Brunswick francophone, had come to Saskatchewan in 1910 to practise law at Vonda and then North Battleford before being appointed a provincial police magistrate for Saskatoon fifteen years later. He was known for his keen wit and his penchant for giving the accused a break. Many first-time offenders who came before him received no more than a harsh tongue-lashing.[12]

Six of the witnesses from the coroner's inquest gave testimony at the preliminary hearing, starting with the provincial pathologist. Leger wanted to hear the whole story and consequently gave Walter Smyth considerable leeway in getting Dr. McGill's evidence entered into the record. But it wasn't long before he clashed with both lawyers.

When Smyth was examining the second witness, farmer John Lee, about his dealings with the Bates, Leger stopped him in mid-sentence with the blunt warning to "get down to evidence now."[13] Ludgate, who had appeared before the magistrate during his police court work, didn't fare much better. While Ludgate and Lee grappled with the question of how long the Bates' car might run on a gallon of gas, Leger had his own brusque answer: "Get an expert."

After an hour-long adjournment for lunch, Leger seemed determined to pick up the pace and refused to let the hearing become bogged down over points of law. Ludgate challenged the admission of the statements that the Bates had given to the mounted police investigators, but Leger just waved his objections away.

Disclosure by the Crown wasn't required at the time, and it might have been the first time that Ludgate had seen the statements when they were introduced into evidence. At the very least, he should have been given the opportunity to question how the confessions had been secured. Police Magistrate Leger, however, was more interested in getting the Bates committed to trial as quickly as possible. Ludgate knew this from his experience in the police courts, and that's why he didn't make a bigger fuss about the admission of the statements. Even then, in the interest of saving time, they were not read aloud.

The magistrate also allowed Constable McLay—again over Ludgate's objection—to repeat what Rose had said after giving her late-night confession: how "she would sleep better now she had it off her mind" and that her husband was "yellow" because he "did not have the guts to kill himself." Corporal Carey, who appeared next, was given similar free rein with his testimony.

The last witness was Patrol Sergeant Williams, who like the others before him essentially repeated what he had earlier told the coroner's inquest. He took great pains, however, to emphasize that the police had been compassionate in their dealings with the couple. When asked directly about his treatment, Williams reported, even Ted said it was "fine." Ludgate was not about to swallow this image of a caring police force and asked the sergeant, "Have you ever heard of an old saying that a person might be killed with kindness?"

"I have, yes," Williams replied. This exchange sent a ripple of laughter through the courtroom. Even Ted cracked a smile.

Leger had heard enough. There would be no stern rebuke from the police magistrate that day. After first warning the Bates, he asked each of them in turn if they had anything to say about the charge they faced. "She has nothing to say," Ludgate replied on behalf of Rose. "I have nothing to say," echoed Ted. Leger then committed the couple to trial the following March on a joint murder indictment. It was 2:45 P.M. It had taken less than four hours, including the lunch break.

Ted and Rose were given fifteen minutes together before they were sent their separate ways: Ted to the Prince Albert provincial jail,

Rose temporarily back to St. Margaret's Hospital. It was a touching moment, with Ted holding his wife's hand as they chatted quietly to one another. The staff reporter for the *Saskatoon Star-Phoenix* was among those moved by the scene. "Their parting," he wrote from Biggar, "indicated that the sordid events of the past week had done nothing by way of lessening mutual affection."[14] Few in the courtroom realized at the time that the loving picture was nothing more than a performance.

CHAPTER SEVEN

BETTER LUCK
THAN US

Ted and Rose Bates were indicted for murder under section 263 of Canada's Criminal Code. By deliberately causing the death of their eight-year-old child, they had committed "culpable homicide."[1] If convicted, they would be sent to the gallows.

It seemed straightforward, at least from a strictly legal perspective. Jackie had died at the hands of his parents on a cold December night in a rural Saskatchewan schoolyard. But there was nothing simple about the case. The prosecution not only had to prove that the couple was guilty of murder, but also had to hope that a jury would be willing to convict them, knowing full well that such a finding would likely result in their execution. The fact that the couple was asserting that the incident was precipitated by the Depression only complicated matters.

There certainly were other options. When first apprised of the crime over the telephone by RCMP corporal Carey, Crown prosecutor Walter Smyth could have recommended that the pair be charged with a lesser crime, such as manslaughter or criminal negligence. It could have still meant prison time for the Bates, but probably would have been regarded as a more reasonable, more just punishment under the circumstances.

Alternatively, Smyth could have sought a psychiatric evaluation of the couple. Rose was clearly a troubled woman. Her desperate pleading with Ted in the car to end her life so that she could join Jackie in death should have raised serious doubts about her sanity. Then, there was her bizarre behaviour while recuperating from her wounds in St. Margaret's Hospital. Rose's stubborn refusal to see her young son one last time, as his body lay in the Biggar morgue, was not normal for a grieving mother. Nor were her intemperate outbursts against her "yellow" husband when she confessed to the mounted police investigators about the death plot. Something was not quite right about her.

Ted, on the other hand, seemed to be in a trance, carelessly oblivious to what he and Rose had done. It could have been the carbon monoxide gas that had dulled his thinking. He had been lying closest to the exhaust pipe in the car that night and was partially paralyzed for several hours. Had he not been, Rose would have been dead too.

Mental capacity was determined by the McNaughton Rules, first adopted in England in 1843 and later incorporated into the Canadian Criminal Code. A defendant could not be held responsible for a crime if he or she was insane at the time of the commission of the offence and did not know the difference between right and wrong. Those found not guilty by reason of insanity would be locked up in an institution. Similarly, a trial could not proceed and the defendant would be institutionalized if he or she did not understand the charges and was therefore unable to assist in his or her defence. Could any of these rules have applied to the Bates?

The Depression could also have been blamed. Ted had stubbornly avoided applying for relief for his family in Vancouver for as long as he could, only to be burdened with the added humiliation of being sent back to Saskatchewan. The thought of facing their former friends in Glidden had apparently been too much for either one of them, or so it seemed. "They were weak and sought the easy way out," is how neighbour George Couper justified their actions.[2]

Those closest to the case, people such as Carey and Smyth, saw things much differently. The Bates had actively plotted the death of their child as part of the suicide pact they had decided upon in Saskatoon. They meant for Jackie to die with them. Their apparent complete lack of remorse only compounded their guilt. It was premeditated murder, and nothing could excuse it, hence the charge.

Getting Ted and Rose to answer for their crime, though, was still three months away. The next sitting of the Court of King's Bench at Wilkie was not expected to begin until mid-March 1934. This delay gave the mounted police and the prosecution plenty of time to put together their case against the couple. Immediately after Magistrate Leger ordered the pair to stand trial, Smyth, Carey, and Corporal Donald McLay huddled in the Biggar RCMP station for about two hours to go over the testimony from both the coroner's inquest and the preliminary hearing and figure out what to do next.

Much of what they talked about doing had already been covered in the days after Jackie's death. They decided to make another visit to the Avalon schoolyard and to check the car again in Saskatoon, especially the engine. They also planned to interview, in some cases for the second time, and take new statements from anyone who had had any dealings with the Bates in Saskatoon. This was standard police procedure. Something new or unexpected might turn up that had been missed the first time.

But Corporal Carey also recommended that the Bates' family life in Glidden and Vancouver be put under a microscope. Rose had taken a liking to the Mountie and privately confided to him in the hospital that married life with Ted "was none too happy."[3] "As a matter of fact," Carey dutifully recorded in his crime report about the conversation, "she told me she would have left her husband years ago ... [but] he would not let her take the child ... that prompted the suicide pact."

Rose's forthrightness cast the incident in an entirely different light. Her comments suggested that the death plot had had more to do with a troubled marriage than the sting of going on relief. In fact, the Depression appeared to be little more than a convenient excuse for the botched murder-suicide. Smyth consequently instructed the police to make some discreet inquiries about the personal lives of the couple. Ted, according to Rose, had been a heavy drinker and gambler during his days as Glidden butcher. That and any other rumours about their lives together in the village needed to be checked out.

Their year in Vancouver, during which time Ted had failed in business three times, also called for examination. Rose had disclosed to Mrs. Kemp, the police matron, that their Kingsway landlord had "told her she could have a home with him any time she desired."[4] Was Rose making it up or did she have an affair right under Ted's nose? Given what the police turned up in Vancouver, there seemed to be some truth in what she was saying. On the evening of 14 December, at the same time that McLay was testifying at the Biggar inquest, RCMP inspector G. W. Fish, accompanied by two constables, called on the Gardiners to see if they had received the three trunks that had been shipped from Saskatoon. Mrs. Gardiner, anxious to cooperate, produced a letter in Rose's handwriting. The postmark indicated that it had been mailed from Saskatoon on 4 December, the day the Bates had headed out on Highway 14 in their rented car. In the note, Rose explained that they were shipping their trunks back to Vancouver and that she hoped that the Gardiners could sell some of the contents to cover the freight charges. If not, they were to ask the Bates' former landlord to pay the bill of lading.

Why, the mounted police wondered, did the couple send their trunks back to Vancouver after they had just paid to ship them to Saskatoon? They would, after all, need them in Glidden—unless they never intended to return to the village. And if the Bates were so desperate for money, then why didn't they just sell some of their belongings?

Hints at what the couple intended to do could also be detected in Rose's letter—phrases like "burn all traces of us", "I cant stand the pressure of it all" and "hope ... you will not be vexed at us."[5] It read as if she was saying her final farewell to some of the few friends that she had left in the world, that she was resigned to her fate. Even then, she wished them a brighter future than Ted and she had known in Canada. "May you have better luck than us," she wrote, as if admitting their failure.

That failure was painfully apparent in another letter that the Gardiners handed over to the police—one they had discovered while going through the household linens and clothing in one of the trunks. It was the heart-rending letter that Rose had addressed to Ted's sister, Lena, sometime before the couple had left for Vancouver. It had never been sent, and now it had fallen into police hands.

"I dont know how to begin," Rose began ominously, "but time as come when I must do so. But I wanted you to know the truth from me not to let Ted tell you just what he liked."[6] The rest of the letter was a rambling indictment of her marriage to Ted, telling how his drinking and gambling had brought them close to financial ruin. "His business is not at all good now," Rose lamented to her sister-in-law, "but its his own fault." The most chilling part was how the couple had quarrelled over custody of their son and how Rose was prepared to take her life and that of Jackie because Ted would not let them leave together. She had reached her breaking point and could see "no way out."

Copies of the two incriminating letters, together with a report about the search of the three Bates' trunks, were forwarded to Smyth and Carey, and to the Attorney General's department in Regina. It was all fodder for the ongoing investigation.

The mounted police, meanwhile, had expanded their search for answers to Perdue. It was here, only hours before the tragedy, that Ted had mailed a letter to Stan Elliot, the Glidden justice of the peace, indicating that he had turned over his interest in the meat market to his sister in England and that they would not be coming back to the village. The Perdue postmaster, Frank Reid, couldn't recall seeing Ted on 4 December, but Der Ying, the operator of the King George Café, remembered serving him coffee and talking about Vancouver. He also said that the man in question had paced nervously and seemed anxious to be on his way, as if he had a place to get to. But when Ying had

WHO KILLED JACKIE BATES?

asked where he was headed, Ted said only a short distance down the road. The police also took a statement from Alcide Belliveau, the local barber who had had a brief conversation with Ted behind the restaurant while the two men smoked. The barber recounted how the stranger, lightly dressed for the weather, wanted to know if there were any abandoned buildings in the area. He seemed to have his mind set on doing something.

This new information strengthened the Crown's case against the Bates. "It would appear," Smyth informed Alex Blackwood, the Saskatchewan Deputy Attorney General, on 18 December, "that the real motive ... may not have had anything whatever to do with relief ... the real motive may be family trouble."[7] The prosecutor drew a direct link between the evidence gathered by the police and the statements provided by the accused. They lined up perfectly with one another, leaving only one possible conclusion. "They actually had the intention of killing this child by the time they left Saskatoon," Smyth insisted, "and ... their actions from that time on were done with the object of fulfilling this intention."

The sticking point, though, was the reliability of the Bates' confessions. During the preliminary hearing, Dr. McGill, the provincial pathologist, had testified that exposure to carbon monoxide would have seriously impaired a person's judgment. If that were the case, then did the Bates really know what they were saying in the days after the incident? The other difficulty was that Ted and Rose had given not one, but two statements. Both initially claimed that the death of Jackie was accidental, but when prodded by the police, they owned up to the suicide pact. Were these contradictory statements attributable to the after-effects of the gas? And were the Mounties out of line when they obtained the second statement?

This last question was raised in a spirited letter that George Couper banged off on the village typewriter to Prime Minister R. B. Bennett, after the Bates had been ordered to stand trial for murder. The Glidden grocer accused the mounted police of harassing Rose in hospital, of visiting her several times late at night in order to secure a confession. He also argued that justice would be served only if the extenuating circumstances were taken into consideration. Couper pleaded for mercy, "Those of us who knew these people, know that their minds had snapped ... these people loved this boy—they worshiped him. He was their only child and had their minds been normal this thing could never have happened."[8]

So, then, were Ted and Rose Bates helpless victims of the relief system, driven by desperation to commit a rash act? Or were they cold-blooded murderers without a bone of regret in their bodies?

That was the problem facing police and the Crown as they decided how to proceed. Smyth and the RCMP might have known the truth behind the boy's death, or at least have had a fairly good idea of what had really happened, but it was even more important to rule out or discredit any other possible explanations for the crime by the time the case went to trial. Any doubt could make a conviction difficult, if not unlikely. The Saskatchewan Department of Justice therefore advised Smyth that its staff lawyers would first review the case to determine whether it indeed warranted the murder indictment. One official even suggested that the Crown would have a greater chance of proving a lesser charge of attempted murder, or perhaps attempted suicide.

The department also decided to find a more senior prosecutor—yet to be identified—to appear alongside Smyth at the trial in the spring. The Biggar lawyer's performance at the coroner's inquest and preliminary hearing had been satisfactory, but not particularly stellar. There were genuine worries that an experienced defence lawyer like Harry Ludgate could easily outfox Smyth, especially given the nature of the crime and the sympathy it was sure to generate. Until then, Department of Justice officials decided to put to rest any doubts that the Bates were not fit to stand trial, and at the same time give Ludgate a little less room to manoeuvre. At the end of the coroner's inquest, the Saskatoon lawyer had asked for a mental examination of his two clients. That request was rejected for some inexplicable reason. The Deputy Attorney General, however, could issue such an order and did so in the week leading up to Christmas.

Ted had been languishing in the Prince Albert provincial jail ever since he had been ordered to stand trial for murder. It was a new facility, barely a decade old, located on Central Avenue at the south end of the future Bryant Park. But the conditions under which he was held made it little better than the old territorial jail it replaced.9

Upon admission on 16 December, Ted was searched, registered, and issued a standard khaki uniform. His hair was also probably cropped short to reduce the spread of vermin, a perennial problem in the jail. His new home was a six-by-ten-foot cell with an eight-foot ceiling in the remand area. Since Ted was awaiting trial and unfamiliar with the prison system, he would have been kept separate and isolated from the general jail population. Indeed, since he had already tried to commit suicide, he would have been watched closely and subject to almost continuous lock-up. As an alleged murderer, and a child killer at that, Ted would likely have been verbally harassed by the staff and other inmates until he was better known and his situation understood. The guards would have ensured, though, that no harm came to him so that he would make his appointment with the hangman, if it ever came to that.

The Prince Albert jail ran on what was known as the silent system. Ted would have been expected to keep quiet at all times unless given permission to speak. And whenever he was addressed by the guards, they would have called him by his prisoner number, P33, never by his name. This loss of identity was compounded by the almost complete lack of contact with the outside world. There were no newspapers, usually just a Bible for reading material, and even that could be taken away as punishment, as was food or the steel bed's mattress. Some prisoners broke under the strain and were shuffled off to the Battleford asylum.

Ted's sanity was put to the test on 2 January 1934, the day after the New Year's holiday. His evaluator was Dr. James Walter MacNeill, medical superintendent of the North Battleford Mental Hospital and a provincial leader in psychiatric treatment. His innovations included removing the bars from the hospital's windows and banning the use of mechanical restraints on patients. MacNeill agreed to do the assessment, but only after the former Glidden butcher had been given a complete physical by the jail surgeon. He also arranged for the laboratory technician at the new Prince Albert Sanitarium to secure a sample of Ted's blood for a Wasserman Test, the standard way to check for syphilis. Once Dr. MacNeill had these reports in hand, he travelled to Prince Albert to interview Bates. His findings were relayed to the Attorney General's department in one simple sentence: "This man is not insane."[10]

MacNeill examined Rose two days later. She was pronounced well enough to be released from the Biggar hospital on Tuesday, 19 December, and was immediately transferred to the provincial Women's Jail in Battleford. The facility had been in operation for only three years. Up to 1930, female offenders had been housed in their own wing at the new Prince Albert jail, but severe overcrowding forced the Saskatchewan government to convert an old Battleford high school into a prison exclusively for women.

At the time of her admission, Rose was one of thirty-seven inmates in a building with only twenty-four makeshift cells. Several women slept on the floor. If that wasn't bad enough, there were no toilets in the cells—just pails that were emptied twice a day. Every evening, after supper, hot water and toilet paper would be passed around as if they were some scarce commodity. In order to keep the vermin under control, the cells, corridors, kitchen, and work areas would be thoroughly washed down with disinfectant once a week. Groups of prisoners were also given baths and a change of clothing on a rotating schedule. In the interim, everyone had their hair regularly combed with coal oil.

The daily routine was equally depressing. All meals were taken in the cells, and the only time the women got outside for some exercise was usually in the late afternoon for half an hour. Days were spent making or mending clothing for other provincial institutions, regardless of one's skill with a needle. At 8 P.M. the matron on duty locked the huge iron gates to the corridors and turned out all the lights.

Rose, prisoner 32 in cell 5, corridor A, had great difficulty adjusting to life behind bars. According to the matron's report books which have survived from this period,[11] she was not sleeping at first and had to be given the barbiturate Luminal. Rose's first Christmas without Jackie was especially hard on her. Unlike the other prisoners who were out of their cells all day, she asked to be left alone. She even took her Christmas dinner in her cell.

Dr. W. A. Kirkpatrick, who attended to the prisoners on a regular basis, prescribed a glass of tonic at the beginning and end of each day. He also apparently left instructions that she be given a sedative whenever necessary—and for good reason. The strain of the past few weeks and months were taking their toll on Rose, who was now a husk of her former self. According to the jail register, she carried only 108 pounds on a five-foot-five frame. She also looked much older than her forty-one years, with her hair more grey than black. The wretched jail conditions didn't help her state of mind or her health, and she probably was only going to get worse.

Just months before Rose was admitted, a pregnant prisoner miscarried and died days later, unattended, in her cell. Although the coroner found the matron-warden's conduct in the matter to be "incredibly cruel," Miss C. C. Faichney was never punished or reprimanded, but continued to enjoy a free hand in the running of the institution.[12] One inmate complained in a letter to a government official, "We are prisoners it is true ... but God never entended for us to be treated like rats or dogs or he would have made us that way instead of women."[13]

Several Doukhobor women, who had been imprisoned for their

nude protests, passively resisted. They went out of their way to defy
the matrons, refusing to go into their cells or to come out, singing for
endless hours, or holding their own religious services. This behaviour,
which often provoked punishment, upset the other prisoners and
added another layer of stress to their lives. Some probably wondered if
they would have been better off in the nearby asylum.

By her second week in jail, Rose was surviving on a steady diet of
Luminal and other drugs. Dr. Kirkpatrick visited her again on New
Year's Eve, a Sunday, this time to take blood for a Wasserman test. Dr.
MacNeill conducted his mental examination shortly thereafter, on 4
January. Something was amiss, though, for the provincial pathologist,
Dr. McGill, made a special trip to Battleford to administer a second
Wasserman test in the early morning of 8 January. The medical records
are silent about the reason.

The criminal investigation, in the interim, was plodding along.
Every detail, no matter how seemingly minor or trivial, was considered.
The police, for example, contacted the Bureau of Vital Statistics in
Regina and secured copies of the Bates' marriage certificate and Jackie's
birth certificate. They also acquired wind and temperature data for the
Biggar–Perdue area the night of the incident.

In Saskatoon, the mounties painstakingly retraced the steps of the
Bates from the time they arrived in the city on 1 December to when
they left three days later on Monday morning. They reinterviewed witnesses, double-checked the family's movements, and generally made
sure that Ted and Rose could have returned to Glidden on the train—
if they had really wanted to. Nothing new turned up, except the fact
that the Bates' trunks, when they were claimed in Saskatoon, were never
opened before they were shipped back to Vancouver.

The police also learned little from poking around in Glidden.
Constable Lambert of the Kindersley detachment tried visiting the vil-
lage before Christmas but had to turn back because of deep snow.
When he finally did make it there on 27 December, the information

he secured by speaking to former neighbours of the family didn't justify taking any statements. It seemed that no one wanted to speak ill
of the Bates, with their fate literally hanging in the balance. "It is generally known that at times the couple would not be on such good
terms," a disappointed Lambert reported, "yet there is nothing ... wor-
thy of remark." Nor was there apparently any truth to the stories that
Rose was seeing other men. "Nothing is known or suspected," he
observed, "that can be regarded as improper."[14]

The findings in Vancouver, on the other hand, revealed the personal turmoil that Ted and Rose were going through before they were sent
back to Saskatchewan as a relief case. The mounted police reinterviewed the Gardiners in the new year and discovered that Rose had
confided to them "she would rather die than return to Glidden." The
Gardiners didn't take the remark seriously at the time, but dismissed it
as "merely a joke."[15]

C. H. "Slim" Babcock, another family friend, told a similar story
to the police. But unlike the Gardiners, he knew that Rose was dead set
against returning to the village *and* meant it. "Mrs. Bates appeared
somewhat downhearted and worried," he recalled in his statement,
"her worry appeared to be very desperate and quite determined."[16]
Babcock also turned over the letter that Ted had sent him from
Saskatoon. The words, "don't think to bad of us if anything should
happen," could not be plainer in the aftermath of the tragedy.[17] As for
Rose's claim that their former landlord, Bob Wolstone, wanted her to
move in with him, Babcock knew nothing of it. In fact, he believed that
there was nothing going on between the pair.

Wolstone said the same thing when he was contacted by the
mounted police. He was quite adamant that he was only trying to help
a family in distress by bringing them groceries and allowing them to be
late with their rent. They were just friends. But if Wolstone was such
a true friend, then why did he give the local newspaper the letter that
Ted had written him just before the couple plunged ahead with their

death pact? The *Vancouver Sun* published it on 7 December 1933 as part of a tell-all exclusive on the Bates' troubled existence in the city. Would he not want to shield his friends in their time of need?

It quickly became apparent, however, during the course of the police interview that Wolstone was really interested only in himself. "Wolstone is of the type that must talk," Detective Sergeant O'Reilly concluded. "If he had any information of value regarding the Bates family, he would be only too willing to broadcast it, feeling that by doing so, he might increase his importance."[18] But Wolstone did not have much to offer the police—nothing that could be considered tantalizing or scandalous about the Bates' private lives. "Their home life was as happy as could be expected considering ... they were destitute," is how the landlord summed up their domestic situation.[19]

The Gardiners and Babcock agreed. They knew nothing about Ted's supposed drinking, gambling, and womanizing, or if they did, they spoke not a word about it. What they did talk about, though, was the Bates' parental love for Jackie. Detective Sergeant O'Reilly ended his report, "All persons ... definitely stated that both the mother and father were very fond of the boy, and looked after him to the best of their ability."[20]

The fact that the RCMP could not find any witness in Glidden or Vancouver who could attest to the Bates' ill-starred marriage did not necessarily weaken the Crown's case against the pair. They still had committed a murder. But the reason for their child's death, according to the statements secured in Vancouver, Saskatoon, and Perdue, seemed to have been the overpowering shame of being sent home to Glidden to secure relief assistance. There was no way that the prosecution would have wanted to put the Depression and the relief system on trial. It would have been like having an elephant in the courtroom, overshadowing the case against the Bates.

Instead, the police, in consultation with the prosecutor, decided to refocus the investigation in January on demonstrating that the child's homicide was premeditated and not an accident. What drove Ted and Rose to commit the crime therefore became less important than the fact that Jackie's tragic death in the back seat of a car in the Avalon schoolyard had been planned. The best evidence in support of a pre-meditation argument was the confessions that Ted and Rose had given to the mounted police in Biggar in the days after Jackie's tragic death. But there were potential problems with this evidence.

George Couper, the Glidden grocer spearheading the Bates' defence fund, had charged that the police had taken advantage of Rose's weakened condition to get a statement out of her. This matter was reviewed by General J. H. MacBrien, the commissioner of the RCMP, who personally assured the justice minister that the Bates had spoken freely to the police after they had been plucked, half-dead, from the car. "It would appear that this complaint is entirely unfound-ed," Commissioner MacBrien argued with an air of authority, "and that every attention, consideration, and courtesy was shown to Mrs. Bates."[21] MacBrien could hardly have been expected to have reported otherwise. He knew from reading the Bates' file, though, that both McLay and Carey had performed their duties scrupulously, a fact con-firmed by the police matron who had kept watch over Rose.

There was still the question of whether the Bates' confessions would be admitted into evidence at the March trial. That issue was helped along by a judgment by Chief Justice J. T. Brown at a sitting of the Saskatchewan Court of King's Bench in Battleford on 28 September 1933. In dealing with a brutal murder by a young man in the Hafford area (R. v. Bohun),[22] Brown had to determine the admissi-bility of several statements, both orally and in written form, that the accused, a nineteen-year-old Ukrainian boy, had given to the police. The chief justice ruled out any written statements because the investi-gating policeman had put down what he wanted the accused to say, not what Bohun actually said. He allowed other statements into evidence, however, because they had been given voluntarily and "not made under fear, not made under compulsion."[23] He made no objection to the number of times the accused had been interviewed as long as the statements recorded every word that had been said.

Chief Justice Brown's decision clearly had a bearing on the forthcoming Bates' trial. It also underscored the importance of securing other evidence. In his oral remarks leading up to his ruling, the chief justice stated that it was a mistake for a police officer to rely solely on a confession to win a case, since the court might see the confession differently. Rather, in Brown's words, "the rule of practice should be to get evidence independent of the statement in order to bring home a conviction."[24] In essence, then, the police had to come up with supporting evidence that Ted and Rose had driven into the Eagle Hills with one purpose in mind: to take their lives and that of their child. They pursued this line of investigation on several fronts.

Ted had claimed when he was first interviewed that he had asked for directions to Rosetown from a man in a wagon on Highway 14 and that he had been instructed to turn north onto the grid road that led to the Avalon school. Corporal Carey spent several frustrating days patrolling the district, trying to find the man in question, if he ever existed. Who would have given such wrong information? It was eventually decided to send a Mountie to the Prince Albert jail in mid-January to interview Ted once again. When asked to describe the man and his outfit, Bates revealed, "I did not speak to any person, I was not telling the truth."[25] He refused, however, to give a written statement to that effect.

The mounted police also tried to determine whether Ted had known about an October 1930 accident in which five men had perished while waiting out a severe snowstorm in their idling car just north of Regina. Perhaps that was where he got the idea about carbon monoxide poisoning. A diligent search was made through the 1930 circulation records of the two Regina daily newspapers, but Ted's name never came up as a subscriber. All the police could say with any certainty was that the five deaths were common talk in Glidden at the time.

A more damning collection of evidence was the five letters that Ted and Rose had written in Saskatoon before they set out in the car Monday morning. These documents clearly showed that the couple was intent on doing something, and that what happened in the schoolyard was not some unfortunate mishap. But here again, there were problems. The police had to prove that the couple had written the letters.

In Ted's case, that was not too difficult. He had signed the register at the Western Hotel in Saskatoon, as well as provided a handwritten confession in the presence of three Mounties and one civilian witness in the Biggar RCMP detachment. There were also the three letters that Ted had written to Stan Elliot in Glidden in the fall of 1933.

Rose, however, had dictated her two statements to Constable McLay in the hospital. The police consequently had to find a way to secure a sample of Rose's handwriting to see if it matched the letter that had been sent to the Gardiners and the letter addressed to Ted's sister that had been found in one of the trunks. Corporal Carey decided to write to Rose at the Battleford Jail and ask whether he could turn over her dead son's clothing to Reverend Kirkbride in Biggar for use by another boy. It was a heartless thing to do, given Rose's fragile state, but the corporal was more concerned with getting a handwriting specimen than protecting her from further grief. Rose replied a few days later, after first getting permission to write the letter. "Any thing of the childs that can be of use to him [Kirkbride] let him have," she pleaded, "just save me his 2 little books he had last and his wrist watch, please."[26]

Carey was initially pleased with himself and how he had managed to get the handwriting sample in such an underhanded way. Then he realized that he would have to prove that Rose was actually the author of the note. Two local Mounties had to be dispatched to the Battleford Jail on 25 January to see whether any staff member had watched Rose write the letter. But the matron-warden had only a vague recollection of having read the letter and was not prepared to swear to it in court. In frustration, the policemen asked to see Rose, who despite being cautioned, confirmed that she had written the letter in question to Carey. She also willingly provided another quick note that was witnessed by both the police and the matron: "This is a sample of my hand writing. Rose Bates."[27]

RCMP superintendent R. R. Tait turned over Rose's note, together with nine other Bates letters, to Thomas Duckworth, an Oxford-trained, Regina-based handwriting expert who was regularly called upon by the police and the justice system for document analysis. It was his job to identify any common features or quirks in the letters, but most important, to determine the authorship.

Collectively, these materials—if it could be firmly established that they were written by Ted and Rose—made a seemingly ironclad case for premeditation. But just to be on the safe side, the Crown prosecutor asked the mounted police to try to locate Ted's older sister Lena. This decision represented a reversal on Walter Smyth's part. When Corporal Carey had earlier recommended that it might be worthwhile to get a copy of the letter that Ted had sent his sister assigning her the outstanding claim to the Glidden Meat Market, Smyth had pooh-poohed the idea. So too had senior Mounties, who were extremely doubtful that anything of importance would be gained by taking the investigation to England. Upon reflection, though, Smyth realized that the letter held out the possibility of further evidence of premeditation. And this was crucial if the police and prosecution were going to make a strong case against the Bates separate and apart from their confessions, as recommended by the chief justice's recent ruling in *R. v. Bohun*.

In late January, then, with the blessing of the Saskatchewan Attorney General's department, RCMP commissioner MacBrien contacted his counterpart at London's New Scotland Yard and asked the British police to track down Ted's sister and to obtain the letter in question. The request was forwarded to the chief constable in Surrey. Days later, Superintendent F. W. Gray and Inspector F. Bishop of the Chertsey Division called on Helena Catherine Butler, a forty-one-year-old war widow and domestic cook living at 201 New Haw Road in Addlestone. Lena was likely shocked when she learned why the police were on her cottage doorstep. She had last heard from her brother in November 1933 when he had sent her the bill of sale and certificate of title to the meat shop.

Lena didn't have much to say about Ted because she really didn't know him. She hadn't seen him in over twelve years and couldn't even provide Rose's maiden name. He was more of a stranger than a brother. Since he had returned to Canada in 1922, Ted had written in late 1925 after Jackie had been born and then not again until June 1932, when he asked to borrow twenty-five pounds. In fact, Lena had been somewhat surprised when she received the deed to the Glidden property—she never expected the loan to be paid back. There was no mention of suicide in the accompanying note. Lena handed over the letters and documents for forwarding to Canada on the understanding that they would be returned to her. She also asked to be informed of the outcome of the trial.

The involvement of Ted's sister was a pathetic footnote to the sorry case. But it had to be done to demonstrate that the couple had no intention of returning to Glidden, even though it was the only place where they would get relief. Ted had nagged Stan Elliot throughout the fall of 1933, imploring his friend to secure the money still owed him from the sale of the meat market, or he would cancel the deal. Then, for some inexplicable reason, he abruptly dropped the matter. It apparently didn't matter any more because he had something else in mind.

Smyth would have to connect the dots at the forthcoming trial, but he would no longer be working the case alone. On 31 January, the Attorney General's department appointed Saskatoon barrister George Arthur Cruise, King's Counsel, to work alongside Smyth as senior Crown prosecutor. For the past quarter century, the fifty-three-year-old Cruise had been practising law in Sutherland, the railway town that was eventually absorbed by Saskatoon. When he wasn't attending to legal affairs, he was working his farm in the present-day Forest Grove neighbourhood, next to the federal tree nursery. Cruise was an experienced prosecutor who had handled a number of trials at which Corporal Carey had testified as the police investigator. But he had an even more direct connection to the Bates case: he had rented the murder car from Bernbaum more than once.

Cruise spent the first week of February ploughing through all the files and evidence. His initial assessment was one of repugnance. "I assure you," he told the Deputy Attorney General, "it does not make very pleasant reading."[28] He was a little more generous in his assessment of Smyth's handling of the coroner's inquest. He called it "a bit cumbersome."[29]

One of the first things that Cruise and Smyth were asked to do was decide on the charge. That wasn't difficult. Both agreed, based on the evidence assembled, that the couple should be tried together for first-degree murder. But how to prove the charge was another matter. In a lengthy letter to Smyth on 7 February, Cruise indicated that he preferred to make the case against the Bates without having to rely on their confessions—something that had been central at the preliminary hearing. He made this suggestion because he suspected that Harry Ludgate, as defence counsel, would play up the Bates' state of mind at the time of the incident. In fact, were Cruise defending the case, he would have laid the blame on Ted in order to exonerate Rose and then tried to "show that his judgment was warped by the distress of the times he was passing through."[30]

Cruise also didn't want to dwell on the reasons why the Bates were reluctant to return to Glidden. He too suspected that the real issue was personal problems between the couple and that the villagers were sitting on some secret. But he also knew that such a line of argument would be an unnecessary distraction. No, just as Smyth himself had realized earlier, Cruise believed that the best approach was to concentrate on proving that "these people set out from Saskatoon to commit the crime with which they are being charged."[31]

Smyth and Carey travelled to Saskatoon on Friday, 16 February, to confer with Cruise about the upcoming trial. They decided to ask the Surveys Branch to make a formal plan of the Avalon school grounds in order to demonstrate that "the place offers no attractions, except to someone minded as these people were." The trio also vigorously debated what witnesses should be called. This process became bogged down because they wanted to bring in several people from as far away as the west coast, and yet they were worried about the expense involved. It would have been far cheaper to build the case around the confessions. Their strategy came into sharper focus after they went over the evidence one more time. They planned to call witnesses from Vancouver, Saskatoon, and Glidden to make the case for premeditation—that the Bates never intended to return to the village even though the Salvation Army had paid for their train tickets.

The key, however, became Perdue. When the family arrived in the village in the early afternoon of Monday, 4 December, Ted and Rose could have changed their minds, could have gone back on their plan. But then, Ted posted the letters. "The die was finally cast," Smyth observed, "and they definitely embarked upon the undertaking which they had contemplated."[32] They drove into the Eagle Hills and that night murdered a helpless child who had drifted off to sleep clutching his two Big Little Books.

CHAPTER EIGHT

THE FIGHT FOR
THEIR LIVES

ight women have been hanged in Canada since 1867. Many more were condemned to death, but their sentences were commuted before their date with the executioner. It seemed that prison time was preferable to capital punishment when it came to women.[1] It was debatable whether Rose Bates would also escape the noose if convicted of first-degree murder. Only one woman, Florence Lassandro, had been sent to the gallows since 1900, and that was in 1923. In fact, right up until she was led to the scaffold for killing an Alberta Provincial Police constable, Lassandro was confident she would be spared because of her gender.[2]

Rose, however, had committed the most heinous of crimes—the premeditated murder of her own child—and not even the extenuating circumstances of the Great Depression might be enough to save her from a possible dance with death at the end of a rope. A murder conviction at the time carried a mandatory death sentence, and only the federal cabinet could spare those found guilty. Perhaps that's why Rose was so fragile. Despite her brave front, especially in dealing with the mounted police, she was probably frightened by the prospect of the Wilkie trial and what a guilty verdict might mean. She was also likely overcome with guilt for what she and her husband Ted had done to their poor son in the Avalon schoolyard.

147

Then, there were the questions that probably haunted her every waking moment. Why had she lived when Jackie had perished? What would have happened to them all if the car hadn't run out of gas? Would she still be alive if Ted hadn't been temporarily incapacitated by the deadly fumes? Why hadn't she said goodbye to Jackie before his funeral?

Rose managed to keep the stress under control with a daily dose of sedatives. It seemed to work reasonably well at first and by early February 1934, according to the matron's report books, she was gradually being weaned off the drugs. But in the early evening of Sunday, 18 February, just after lights out, she had a sharp pain in her chest that lasted several minutes. It could have been nothing more than a panic attack, a mild heart attack at worst. Rose attributed the episode to the way she had been lying in bed and was feeling better the next morning. One week later, though, coincidentally on another Sunday evening, she had a second attack, this time more debilitating than the first one. She felt nauseated from the pressure around her heart, and it was only after she vomited up her supper that the pain went away. Rose had apparently recovered enough to be back at work two days later, but at a different job in the jail—ironing. It seemed to have a calming effect on her, and with the help of drugs there were no more attacks.

It wasn't until 11 March, however, that she was finally examined by the jail doctor during one of his visits. Dr. Kirkpatrick checked her heart and blood pressure, as well as conducted some mental tests. His findings are not known, but Rose was evidently pronounced well enough to go to trial for murder. There is no mention of her again in the matron's notebooks until the following Saturday, three days before she was scheduled to go on trial in Wilkie, when she was found sitting up in her cell at midnight and given two sleeping pills. Rose got the same dosage the next evening before she went to bed. She probably slept through the meteor that roared across the night sky and rattled doors and windows as it disintegrated over Saskatchewan and Alberta. It could have been an omen.

RCMP constable A. L. Seaman and police matron Dorothy Barr picked up Rose at the jail early on Monday, 19 March. It had been exactly three months to the day since her admission, and her long wait to learn her fate would be over soon. Since there was no rail line from Battleford south to Wilkie, Rose and her two escorts rode east on the CN line to Saskatoon and then doubled back on the CP line to Wilkie. Highways were not ploughed in winter, and train travel was more reliable, even if it added more miles to the trip.

Ted Bates arrived in Wilkie that same day along with Corporal Charles Carey and Constable Donald McLay. He had been taken first from Prince Albert to Saskatoon over the weekend and then to Biggar on Monday morning, where he was handed over to the custody of the two police investigators. All three men then travelled by train to Reford, a rural siding on the CN line just south of Wilkie, where they were met by a waiting squad car.

Little is known about Ted's time in the Prince Albert jail. His lawyer, Harry Ludgate, visited him at least once, probably in early February after George Cruise had been appointed senior Crown prosecutor in the case. Dr. J. W. MacNeill of the North Battleford Mental Hospital also made a special trip to the jail in mid-March to make a second assessment of Ted's fitness for trial. It is not clear who made the request, let alone why. There is no mention in the North Battleford records of MacNeill examining Rose again.

Rose and Ted were joined in Wilkie by thirty-one witnesses who had been subpoenaed to give evidence. It appears that the prosecution team had had second thoughts about trying to keep the trial costs down, especially if the savings came at the expense of winning the case. Cruise and his prosecution partner Walter Smyth also wanted to leave no doubt in the minds of the jury that the killing of Jackie Bates had been carefully calculated by his parents and that Rose had been talking about ending her life even before the family was forced to return to Saskatchewan. Over one hundred dollars was consequently spent to bring the Bates' friends, Slim Babcock and Ruby Gardiner, from Vancouver. Cruise believed that their testimony "might give finish to the case."[3]

All of the local witnesses were expected to get to the trial on their own. Several people, however, simply didn't have the money because of the heavy hand of the Depression. Stan Elliott, for example, complained to the Mounties in early March that he couldn't afford the fare from Glidden to Wilkie and that he had no funds for subsistence once he got there. The Kindersley RCMP detachment advanced him twenty dollars.

Harry Ludgate also found himself in an embarrassing predicament. When the Saskatoon barrister agreed to represent the Bates at the coroner's inquest and preliminary hearing, the Glidden village council had assured him that his services would be covered by a special defence fund raised through public subscription. And George Couper, as secretary for the fund, set out to do just that—in his words, "help these unfortunate people in the fight for their lives."[4] Throughout December and January, Couper sent letter after letter to railway station agents, urging them to canvas their communities for donations to the Bates trust fund. "If this was an ordinary cold-blooded murder," he explained, "our citizens would have let matters take their course, but when decent citizens have been face to face with starvation through no fault of their own we feel public opinion can best assert itself by providing adequate defence."[5]

To Ludgate's chagrin, though, the appeal for donations had unfortunately come up empty. By the end of February 1934, there wasn't even any money to cover the services he had already rendered. Ludgate decided to write the Saskatchewan government, less than two weeks before the start of the trial, asking the Attorney General's department to appoint him defence counsel for the Bates. "This, I think," he reasoned, "is in the interests of the accused themselves and of justice generally speaking."[6] Alex Blackwood, the Deputy Attorney General, neatly sidestepped the request by advising Ludgate that the matter would have to be taken up with the trial judge. He was the one who was authorized to appoint defence counsel in such cases.

But who was going to preside over the controversial trial? That was one of the most talked-about topics in the Saskatchewan legal community in the late winter of 1934. There was no shortage of speculation or gossip. George Cruise actually raised the matter one day in casual conversation with Justice Donald MacLean. He told MacLean that he was worried that it might be "difficult ... to get the judge and jury to do their part" and wondered aloud who had been given the nod to handle the Bates trial.7 MacLean didn't answer the question directly, but insisted that the Wilkie court could not escape its duty. "If the evidence were such that the accused had committed the crime of murder," MacLean studiously maintained, as if he was rendering a judgment, "it would be the duty of the jury so to find and of the judge to pass the death sentence."8

These remarks didn't necessarily ease Cruise's concerns. Rather, they served to remind him that the prosecution faced an onerous task—something he communicated to Smyth in the weeks winding down to the trial. "We must consider ourselves tied by a sense of duty," Cruise observed, "no matter how our sentiment may run as to those who brought about the death of an innocent child."9

They would get that chance to do their duty when the regular sitting of the Court of King's Bench opened in Wilkie on Tuesday, 20 March, at 10 A.M. The courthouse was an old three-storey frame school that had been converted into the judicial center for the district. The presiding judge was Hector Y. MacDonald.

Born on Cape Breton Island and of Highland Scottish, Roman Catholic origin, the fifty-eight-year-old MacDonald had practised law in Nova Scotia before heading west to Saskatchewan in 1906. Twelve years later, after several years in private practice as a litigator, he was appointed to the Court of King's Bench. Justice MacDonald, often described as astute and sharp-witted, had a commanding grasp of the law, which he administered without equivocation. By coincidence, the first person he sentenced to death was a woman. MacDonald had no use for extraneous testimony and was often quick with his decisions. He could also be mischievous at times. He used to take great delight in interrupting future prime minister John Diefenbaker just as the Prince Albert lawyer was taking full flight in his concluding address to the jury.

When MacDonald opened the proceedings that March morning, he looked out onto a packed room, including six young women standing at the back of the court, vigorously chewing gum in anticipation of what was going to unfold. The "Depression Slaying," as it was being dubbed in the newspapers, promised to be one of the most sensational things to happen recently in the sleepy CPR divisional point of twelve hundred people. But any interest in the grisly story and the fate of the Bates couple was largely local. None of the country's major newspapers had a reporter in the courtroom, preferring to rely on the wire services for information about the trial. Nor did the incident cause a ripple in either Ottawa or Regina. It seemed to be just another Depression story.

The Bennett government was busy grappling with the larger problem of the single, homeless unemployed and the challenge of getting the country back on the road to economic recovery. The plight of the Bates didn't even merit a mention in the acrimonious House of Commons debate over a new relief bill. The same week as the trial, the prime minister was quoted as saying that "the dole creates a race of parasites."[10] Contrast that with an Edmonton news story at the time that reported that almost two thousand primary school children in the city were undernourished because their parents refused to apply for relief.

The Anderson government, meanwhile, was trying to limit the damage the Depression had wrought to its credibility before it went to the Saskatchewan electorate later that year. The last thing it wanted on its hands was any connection to the Bates story. Curiously, though, Jimmy Gardiner, the rough-and-tumble former Liberal premier and leader of the Opposition at the time, chose not to exploit the government's vulnerability over the incident, not even for partisan purposes. The Bates story doesn't even appear in his voluminous correspondence.

Gardiner, however, probably had an opinion on the case, as did many other Saskatchewan people. And that was one of the first challenges at the trial: selecting twelve impartial men from among the Wilkie citizens who had been called for jury duty. Harry Ludgate, who had been assigned by Judge MacDonald to defend the Bates, turned away twelve men. Walter Smyth, representing the Crown, asked another eight to step aside. It took almost until noon to complete the process. Even then, there was whispering about the jury's objectivity. RCMP patrol sergeant Williams, in speaking to local people about the case, found that "no one wanted the accused to be found Guilty, although the general opinion was that they were Guilty."[11] George Cruise had a similar experience. While the trial was underway, a Wilkie lawyer told him that "he knew two men on the jury who declared they would not convict."[12]

The twelve jurors were numbered in the order they were empanelled: 1. Walter Taylor; 2. G. B. Warburton; 3. Matthew A. E. Clements; 4. James B. Laidlaw; 5. O. O. Golberg; 6. William Rudd; 7. A. E. Cockburn; 8. Charles H. Miller; 9. Edgar Howard Dulmage; 10. John Sherwood; 11. Clarence E. Halliday; 12. John Thorpe. Their occupations, known for only about half of them, ranged from farmer and drayman to mechanic, grocer, and hardware merchant.[13] Art Edwards, the principal of McLurg School, served as court reporter.

The first witness that afternoon was Stan Elliot, long-time Glidden friend of the Bates family. He talked about the family, how long he had known them, and how he had handled the sale of the Glidden meat market. He then explained under questioning how Ted had written him three times from Vancouver in the fall of 1933, each

WHO KILLED JACKIE BATES?

time imploring him to collect the $450 outstanding balance or to repossess the business. That much was understandable for a man down and out on his luck, trying to keep his family off relief in Vancouver. But then Elliot talked about a fourth letter, dated 2 December in Saskatoon, that had been mailed to him from Perdue according to the postmark. It was the letter in which Ted had mysteriously turned over his interest in the meat shop to his sister in England. Even more puzzling, though, was his comment that the family had been headed back to Glidden only to change their mind.

C. H. "Slim" Babcock, one of the two Vancouver prosecution witnesses, was called next. He described how his friend Ted had been forced to apply for relief, only to be turned away because he had not lived in Vancouver for at least a year. If that wasn't bad enough, Babcock recounted, officials then informed Ted that the family had to return to Saskatchewan. The news could not have been more devastating after what they had been through. Rose found it all terribly unfair and vowed never to return to Glidden—she would rather kill herself. These words created quite a stir in the courtroom, but Babcock put Rose's outburst down to shame. The shame of being destitute in Vancouver. The shame of being denied relief. The shame of being sent back to Glidden, where the whole town would know about their failure. There would be no escape for the Bates unless they could obtain relief in Saskatoon or some other place in Saskatchewan.

Ludgate tried to blunt the impact of the testimony by establishing from the outset that the Bates were loving parents whose world had been turned upside down by the Depression. He got Babcock to admit, "I never saw a mother more devoted to a son in my life."[14] But then, with great flourish, Babcock added that Rose looked "like a prisoner going into an exile in hell" when she learned that the family was being sent back to Glidden as a relief case.

Ruby Gardiner, Rose's only female friend in Vancouver, provided further damning evidence. She reported that the Bates had shipped back to Vancouver the three trunks that they had taken to Saskatoon at their own expense. And, from the letter the Gardiners had received from Rose, it appeared that they had been sent back before the family had left the city in the rented car. Ludgate ignored the testimony, concentrating instead on what Mrs. Gardiner could tell the court about the relationship between Jackie and his parents. She confirmed what Babcock had said before her: they were doting parents who loved their son dearly.

The prosecution then shifted the case to Saskatchewan and went over much of the same evidence from the coroner's inquest and preliminary inquest, only this time the witnesses included people from Perdue and the questioning was done by George Cruise. Ted, sitting upright in the prisoner's dock, followed the testimony with great interest, almost as if he were hearing it for the first time. Rose, on the other hand, seemed embarrassed by it all and sat with her head lowered for most of the afternoon.

At 6 P.M., with Constable McLay less than halfway through his evidence, Judge MacDonald decided to adjourn proceedings and sent the jury off to be sequestered for the night. It had been a long first day, but the trial promised to be short. Eighteen prosecution witnesses had appeared that afternoon, and there were only another thirteen waiting in the wings for their turn in the witness box.

It had not been a stellar performance, however, for the prosecution team of Cruise and Smyth. Sure, they had introduced new evidence that the Bates were contemplating something terrible before they left Vancouver, but that same evidence also suggested that the Depression and Canada's relief policies had played a deciding role in the boy's death. Ludgate must have been smiling to himself.

When the trial resumed the next morning at ten o'clock, the jury was unexpectedly absent. Judge MacDonald explained to the court that the defence had asked for, and been granted, an opportunity to challenge the admissibility of the Bates' confessions before McLay continued with his testimony. Ludgate began rather dryly with legal argument. He said that it was one of the principles of law that neither husband nor wife could be called upon to incriminate one another. The Saskatoon lawyer also cited several cases involving the questioning of accused persons, in particular the ruling of British jurist Lord Cave who said that a policeman should keep his mouth shut and his ears open. Cruise countered that Saskatchewan courts seemed to think otherwise, noting that the statements of accused murderer William Bahrey had been accepted at his recent trial.[15]

Ludgate then questioned several witnesses about how the confessions had been secured. He forced McLay to account for each time Rose had been interviewed at the hospital before demanding to know whether the mounted police really had the permission of the doctor to be there. He then went after Corporal Carey, who claimed that Rose had volunteered to tell the police everything. He wanted to know who had authorized the late-night hospital visits to the sick woman.

Ludgate, in a fighting mood, turned next to police matron Mrs. P. Kemp and asked whether in good conscience she could corroborate the testimony provided by McLay and Carey. She did that and more. Kemp was not only present each time Rose was interviewed by the Mounties, but she quoted her as saying, "I know we will hang, we deserve it."[16] The remarks caught Rose by surprise, and she looked up suddenly from the prisoner's dock as if she had been stung.

Rose would get her chance to respond when Ludgate called her to the witness stand. All eyes in the court seemed fixed on her as she took her place in the box, refusing the offer of a chair. Rose spoke in a quiet, almost hushed, voice, forcing people to strain to hear her every word. But there was nothing reticent about her testimony. What exactly did Constable McLay say, Ludgate asked, when he came to the hospital? He said, she responded, "It will be easier for you and easier for me if you make a statement."[17] And what did Mrs. Kemp say when I asked her to swear to that? "No, Harry," Rose recounted, "this job is my bread and butter. I can't afford to quarrel with the police."

Judge MacDonald stuck his oar in at this point, and in his high-pitched voice asked Rose whether she had known that she was not obliged to make any statement. She said yes, but had decided to talk to the police after she learned that her husband had reportedly told them everything.

Ludgate's final witness was Dr. Brace, the Biggar physician who had treated the couple. He described Rose's wounds and her generally poor physical condition. He also couldn't remember giving the police approval to interview her. He would have made them wait at least three or four days.

"Was she all right mentally?" the judge interjected.[18] Brace said she was fine, that she would understand what she was saying to the police, but he was worried about her overall weakened state. Ludgate then argued against the admission of the statements, insisting that Rose had been induced by the police to give information at a time when she was vulnerable.

"Can you give me any authority," quizzed MacDonald, "which says it is wrong to advise a person that it is better to tell the truth?"[19] Ludgate replied that the law found it wrong if the person being interviewed was excited or nervous. But that applied, the judge shot back, only to the weight given to statements, not their admissibility. Ludgate wasn't about to give up and hurriedly began to recite his arguments again, almost sputtering as he tried to make his points. The judge, however, just held up his hand and ruled that the statements could be admitted because they had been given voluntarily.

The jury filed back into the courtroom at 11:15 A.M. Despite the late start in hearing the first evidence of the day, there was still the prospect that the prosecution could wrap up its case by the end of the day, especially since much of it was a repetition of the December proceedings. Constable McLay took his place in the witness stand and resumed his testimony from the previous afternoon. He described in detail how the

Bates had attempted to kill themselves and their son in the Avalon schoolyard. The only time he stumbled, seemingly upset, was when he talked about Jackie reading the *Mickey Mouse* and *Chester Gump* books in the back of the car.

McLay then began to read the Bates' statements aloud. He stopped at one point and related how he asked Ted why he had cleaned the blood from the knife that he had used to hack away at Rose's neck. "I'm a butcher, you know," Ted was said to have explained.[20] It was Rose's statement, however, that was the real shocker of the two. Where Ted had been mercifully brief, his wife recalled their death pact in all its horror. People in the courtroom sat there stunned, many with their mouths open, as McLay read the gruesome account of the couple's desperate struggle to end their lives. The exclamation point was what Rose had said to the policemen after giving her statement. McLay told the court that she blamed Ted for the poor job he had done in trying to cut his wrists: "He was too yellow. He didn't have guts enough."[21] Rose reacted by shaking her head in disbelief, seemingly regretting her words.

Cruise then produced the heavy car crank that Ted had used to try to bash the back of his wife's head. McLay dutifully identified it, while many in the courtroom twisted in their seats to get a better look. Ludgate had only one question for the constable: Who gave him permission to visit Rose in hospital? McLay claimed that he would never have interviewed the injured woman unless it was okay to do so.

Corporal Carey followed. Cruise had worked with the Mountie on a number of previous cases and considered his court work to be "consistent and reliable."[22] But before Carey got very far into his evidence, Ludgate interrupted to inform Judge MacDonald that his sole defence witness, Dr. W. D. McPhail of Kindersley, had been summoned home on a medical emergency. McPhail had arrived in dramatic fashion in Wilkie earlier that day by airplane. He told the judge that he could fly back to Kindersley to perform the operation and return for his court appearance within three hours. Cruise didn't see a problem in excusing

THE FIGHT FOR THEIR LIVES

the doctor since he didn't expect to complete his examination of all the prosecution witnesses that afternoon.

Once this commotion was over, Carey resumed his testimony, essentially repeating what he had told the coroner's inquest and preliminary hearing in December. It was all fairly straightforward. Ludgate, though, was lying in wait. In his cross-examination, he asked if the corporal had ever written Mrs. Bates while she was being held in the Battleford Women's Jail. Carey said yes, that he wanted to know what should be done with the dead boy's clothing. Ludgate scoffed at the explanation, intimating that there was another reason for the letter. A somewhat chastened Carey admitted that there was a double purpose—he also wanted to secure a sample of Rose's handwriting.

The Saskatoon lawyer then wondered if the simple act of operating a car might result in the inhalation of carbon monoxide. Carey responded that he had driven thousands of miles and was never aware of any such danger. "You don't know there's any danger when you're dying," quipped the judge.[23] The court erupted in laughter.

Mrs. Kemp appeared next and repeated the evidence she had given earlier in the day when the jury was excluded. So too did Dr. Brace when his turn came. This time, however, the physician was a little more forthcoming, suggesting that Mrs. Bates had problems with depression.

"Is that a form of insanity?" innocently asked Cruise, who didn't seem to realize the minefield he was entering.[24]

"You might call it a border line form," Brace answered. "I think her age has quite a bit to do with [it], being in the climacterium or change of life ... Worry brought her down to that condition of physical and mental debility. Failure to sleep well, eat well, irritability and general nervousness were signs ... Uncontrollable acts might result in extreme cases." But, continued the prosecutor, would Mrs. Bates be victimized by these so-called uncontrollable acts? She might, answered the doctor.

Ludgate gladly charged through the opening provided by Cruise.

He asked whether Rose was in any condition to answer questions when she was first hospitalized. No, she was not fit, glumly replied Brace, and he would not have given the police permission to talk to her. Nor did he think the nurse or matron was qualified to make such a decision. In fact, Brace contended that the stress of the constant interviewing probably kept Rose in hospital longer than she should have been.

Judge MacDonald called a fifteen-minute recess before Dr. Frances McGill, the provincial pathologist, entered the witness box. She carefully reviewed her autopsy of "the plump little boy" and how her findings pointed to carbon monoxide poisoning as the unmistakable cause of his death. When Cruise asked about Jackie's history of fainting, McGill simply observed, "Many boys, normal boys, have fainting spells."[25]

The Bates tried to keep their emotions in check as best they could as McGill outlined her probing of their son's organs. Rose sat there quietly weeping, chewing on her fingers, while Ted looked off into the distance, as if he were somewhere else, any place but there.

There was more to come, though. Cruise held up the two knives, two razor blades, and three towels that had been found inside the car. All the items, according to McGill, had tested positive for human blood, the Bates' blood. Rose tried to shut out the harrowing memory raised by the exhibits by keeping her head down with her hands pressed against her face. Ted, with his forehead wrinkled, seemed lost in thought, perhaps recalling what he had done in his gas-induced daze the night of Jackie's death. The scars on his wrist would never let him forget.

The graphic medical evidence was certainly hard to refute, especially since it was backed by McGill's standing as one of the country's foremost criminal pathologists. After all, she had solved many more difficult or mysterious cases. This one pointed to a botched murder-suicide. Ludgate, however, was ready to square off against the doctor on her own turf and launched into an eighty-minute, scientific cross-examination that was exhausting in its intensity. All the while, he was actively coached by Dr. McPhail, whose errand of mercy to Kindersley had never materialized and who was there at Ludgate's elbow, suggesting questions to throw at the pathologist.

Ludgate began by asking McGill if there could have been any other cause or contributory cause in the boy's death. Was that possible? She emphatically said no, the post-mortem examination left no doubt that the child had died from carbon monoxide poisoning. He then led McGill through her autopsy report, pausing here and there to ask questions about her examination of the dead boy's body. He also confirmed that McGill had never inspected the car involved in the incident, nor at any time had asked to see it.

Ludgate's next series of questions seemed designed to test McGill's knowledge of status lymphaticus.[26] This so-called disease had its origins in the late nineteenth century when the medical profession was trying to find a natural cause for unexpected death in otherwise healthy children and young adults. The trigger, according to a Viennese doctor, was an enlarged thymus gland, a lymphatic organ in the throat. Pressure from an enlarged thymus could inhibit respiration and lead to sudden death. By 1911, status lymphaticus was accepted in Great Britain as an official cause of death. The fatal disease also found its way into medical textbooks and was often associated with pale, flabby children with enlarged tonsils and adenoids. Indeed, it was recommended that the thymus be removed or irradiated. Pathologists, however, dismissed the condition as sheer quackery, for the simple reason that the thymus gland is normally large in infants and gradually diminishes in size as the child ages.

Confronted with these conflicting views, the Medical Research Committee of Great Britain conducted a thorough review of status lymphaticus deaths throughout the 1920s and announced in 1931 that there was no such disease. It never existed, except in the minds of those troubled by unexplained death. But the diagnosis did not disappear until after the Second World War, when the disease was finally dropped from textbooks and a new generation of doctors found other, more plausible causes for sudden death in children. In other words, status lymphaticus was still very much part of the medical vocabulary when the Bates went on trial in Wilkie for the death of their son.

Ludgate pressed Dr. McGill to explain to the court if she had given any special attention to the thymus during her autopsy of Jackie's body. The pathologist reported that she had done only a quick visual inspection of the gland. She had neither sectioned it nor looked at a tissue sample under a microscope. How then could she rule out status lymphaticus as a possible cause of death, questioned the Saskatoon lawyer?

These words were akin to waving a red flag in front of a bull. An irritated McGill, making no attempt to hide her derision, informed Ludgate that Jackie's thymus, although large, was not abnormal. But wasn't a large thymus a telltale sign of the disease? persisted Ludgate. The doctor brusquely retorted that status lymphaticus was pure nonsense, a bogus theory lamely put forward by doctors to cover up their ignorance of human anatomy. Ludgate cut her off at that point, indicating that the defence would be introducing evidence to the contrary. Dr. McGill completed her testimony at 5:50 P.M., prompting Judge MacDonald to adjourn the proceedings until the following morning when the last two prosecution witnesses would be heard.

Anyone scoring the trial that second day would have given the edge to the prosecution—that is, up until Ludgate raised the prospect of some cause other than carbon monoxide poisoning in Jackie's death. He effectively caught the prosecution by surprise and piqued the interest of those watching the trial. Like any good defence lawyer, though, he was more interested in the impact it might have on the members of the jury, if only on one of them.

The prosecution tried to regain the upper hand the next morning, Thursday, 22 March, by first having Constable McLay identify the two children's books found in the death car, calling and formally entering them as exhibits. The message could not have been more transparent: these people were child killers.

Cruise then called Dr. J. W. MacNeill, superintendent of the North Battleford Mental Hospital. It was a bizarre move on Cruise's part, one that even Judge MacDonald privately chastised him for after the trial. Normally, the matter of an accused's sanity would be raised only by the defence. Besides, the psychiatrist's testimony could absolve Rose of any responsibility because of her fragile mental state. But Cruise knew from his discussions with MacNeill that Rose was a troubled woman long before the Depression came along and that her behaviour had nothing to do with how the family had been treated by the relief system. And he was prepared, in his words, to have "the whole thing set before the court."[27]

Ludgate, however, objected to Dr. MacNeill's appearance on the grounds that the question of the defendants' sanity had never been formally raised by the Crown. He was obviously worried that if Rose were found to be mentally unstable, then the blame could be pinned on Ted alone. Besides, he was gunning for an acquittal for both of them and had decided to take the all-or-nothing route on the murder charge. Judge MacDonald acknowledged the objection but allowed MacNeill to take the witness stand on the understanding that any evidence was to be restricted to the doctor's recent psychiatric assessment of the Bates. It was a frustrating ruling—Cruise later called it a "petty objection"—but the prosecution was confident that MacNeill's testimony could still help make the case for premeditation.[28]

Cruise got right to the heart of the matter and asked about the doctor's findings about the Bates. "I think they're not insane," MacNeill declared.[29] He then went on to explain why. He found Ted perfectly sane, while Rose suffered from what he described as "a case of anxiety neurosis." She had been traumatized by some incident at the age of twenty-four—sometime during the Great War—and had never recovered from the shock. It could have been the death of a loved one. Private Thomas Slatter (her second oldest brother was named Tom) died on 28 April 1917, two days after Rose's birthday. It's not possible, though, to confirm his identity because the dead soldier's age is unknown. MacNeill was prohibited from saying more about Rose's past history because of MacDonald's ruling, but he did add that irritability and obsessions were some of the symptoms associated with her neurosis.

Cruise then questioned whether Rose's anxiety had anything to do with what had happened to the family in Vancouver. MacNeill said that the family's failure to secure relief would have aggravated, not caused, her condition. He also maintained, in a thinly veiled reference to the McNaughton Rules, that Rose would have known the difference between right and wrong and that any acts would have consequences. Ludgate asked only one question in his cross-examination. He wondered how Rose's apparent condition might have affected her husband. MacNeill replied that Ted could have "followed the line of least resistance."[30]

The last prosecution witness was Thomas Duckworth, a Regina handwriting expert. He had prepared a photographic chart of several of the Bates' letters in order to identify commonalities in the penmanship styles. But before Duckworth was able to discuss his findings, the judge ordered him to cut off the letter that Rose had written to Carey from the Battleford Jail. He also excluded, at Ludgate's urging, Rose's heart-rending 1932 letter to her sister-in-law that had been found in one of the trunks sent to the Gardiners. MacDonald considered it irrelevant to the case, even though Rose threatened to take her life and that of Jackie to escape her marriage with Ted. In his testimony, Duckworth drew attention to a number of common characteristics in the letters on his chart and concluded that they had been written by only two people. He also speculated that the two letter-writers were from the Old Country because of the handwriting styles, but that one person was clearly better educated than the other.

That concluded the Crown's case, and Judge MacDonald called on the defence to call its only witness: Dr. Wilburn Darley McPhail.[31] McPhail was something of a local legend. Born in Ontario but raised in Winnipeg, Barney, as he was popularly known, served in the RAF during the Great War before completing his medical degree at the University of Manitoba. McPhail opened a practice in Kindersley in 1928 and came to epitomize the small-town doctor, the kind who made house calls at all hours of the day or night. But it was his swashbuckling style that made him stand out. Robust in appearance and forthright in his views, he dominated anything he became involved in by sheer force of personality. He also had a reputation for being "quick with the knife."[32]

How McPhail became hooked up with Ludgate is not known, but the lawyer probably encountered him during his preparation for the trial—Jackie Bates had once been McPhail's patient. Ludgate obviously liked what he had heard, and in his affidavit requesting that McPhail be subpoenaed for the trial, he claimed that the doctor was "a necessary and material witness ... without whose evidence I cannot safely conduct the defence."[33]

McPhail seemed determined to live up to this assessment and delivered quite a performance. He even came with props. In taking his place in the witness box, he and Ludgate stacked seventeen large medical books along the railing for handy reference. Ludgate asked McPhail if he had heard the testimony of Dr. Brace and Dr. McGill from the previous day. He confirmed that he had and added that the police should not have interviewed Mrs. Bates for at least three or four days.

The questioning then turned to his relationship with the victim. McPhail reported that he had examined Jackie in 1928 and 1929 at the request of his father. The boy had been experiencing frequent fainting spells, a persistent cough, and difficulty swallowing. McPhail attributed these problems to septic tonsils and adenoids, but the real threat to the boy's health was an enlarged thymus. He recommended radiation treatment, but the family never pursued it, probably because of the expense.

Ludgate wanted to know more about thymus death, and McPhail was only too happy to oblige. He picked up Osler and McCrae's *Modern Medicine* and read several passages linking a large thymus to sudden death. For the benefit of the court, he said it was like driving a speeding car, slamming on the brakes, and killing the engine. McPhail talked about studies of the disease, including the mortality rates, dipping into the books before him every now and again. It took him almost fifteen minutes to find one reference—a visibly annoyed Cruise was timing him! He stopped at one point to ask whether it was necessary to keep repeating that the books he was quoting from were standard texts in the field. "We don't expect they will go out of date while you are giving evidence," said MacDonald, smiling.[34]

McPhail claimed that Jackie had the telltale signs of a "lymphatic constitution." The boy was flabby, pale, effeminate—or "a sissy," interjected the judge. And unless the dead child's thymus was more fully examined, McPhail asserted, it was impossible to be certain about the cause of death. "The autopsy was therefore incomplete," he decreed.[35]

Judge MacDonald decided to call a lunch break at this point. The timing could not have been better for the local reporters who now had their headline for the late edition of their newspapers. The *Saskatoon Star-Phoenix* reported "Enlarged Gland May Have Killed Boy, Doctor Says," while the *Regina Leader-Post* was a little more circumspect: "Other Causes in Bates' Lad Death Sought."[36]

When court resumed at two o'clock, McPhail continued to chip away at the autopsy report. He more or less insinuated that Dr. McGill had been negligent in failing to conduct several essential pathological tests. He chided her, for example, for not determining the exact percentage of carbon monoxide in the boy's blood.

"Could long exposure on a cold night, coupled with a thymus condition ... cause death?" Ludgate asked in summation.

"Yes," the witness replied.[37]

Ludgate then stepped aside for Cruise, who was anxious to have a crack at Dr. McPhail. The lead prosecutor first asked about the cherry red colour of Jackie's blood and whether it was an indication of carbon monoxide poisoning. McPhail said it might be, but it could also be the result of other causes.

"We can't go through a whole school of medicine in this court," an exasperated MacDonald erupted.

Cruise asked his question again. "My opinion," McPhail resolutely stated, "is that the boy died from a hyper-active thymus poisoning." Then how did he account for the reaction of Ted and Rose to the gas, parried Cruise. The cold, McPhail countered, could cause vomiting.

"Is there anything in the autopsy report inconsistent with carbon monoxide poisoning?" lamented his lordship.

"I can't say that there is," grumbled McPhail, but "the report is insufficient."[38]

The doctor vacated the witness box at 3:30 P.M. Ludgate then formally announced that the defence rested its case. The words were barely out of his mouth, however, when Cruise recalled Dr. McGill as a rebuttal witness for the Crown. The pathologist had sat quietly in court for several hours while McPhail called into question her professionalism and her expertise. She was more than ready to trade jabs. "The thymus gland was perfectly normal in every appearance," she stated sarcastically. "If we took sections of all parts of the body it would take two years. I might as well have taken a cross-section of the big toe."

McGill also raised doubts about the doctor's knowledge of human anatomy. She skewered him for incorrectly locating the position of the thymus during his testimony. But she reserved her most devastating comments for his criticism of her blood work. McGill called carbon monoxide "a most deadly poison" because of how it bonded so closely with oxygen in the blood. It would take only 1 per cent of the gas to kill a person. But in Jackie's case, she found a range of 25 to 40 per cent carbon monoxide in his blood ten days after his death. Ironically, this test had been requested by Ludgate after he agreed to serve as the Bates' defence counsel. "Carbon monoxide was the cause of death without any doubt whatsoever," the pathologist thundered so there would be no misunderstanding.[39]

Ludgate was then given an opportunity to ask questions. He wondered why McGill hadn't brought any authorities to court to back up her statements as the defence witness had done. "Are you sure this diagnosis was not arrived at by you before you left Regina?" he charged.

"No, decidedly not," McGill reacted angrily. She repeated that the boy's thymus was normal and that the diagnosis of status lymphaticus was hogwash.

"There's an old saying," Ludgate offered, "that doctors differ and patients lose their lives."

Before McGill had time for a comeback, Judge MacDonald added, "Yes and lawyers differ and patients lose their lawsuits."[40]

There was a ten-minute adjournment before the two sides gave their closing addresses. Ludgate spoke for just seven minutes. He talked about the gravity of the case, how it was "a doubly serious murder charge" because the lives of two people hung in the balance. He also emphasized how the jury had to be satisfied that the couple was guilty, and that unless they did the right thing, they could face "wakeful nights when it was too late to correct a mistake."

To help the jurors make their decision, Ludgate reminded them that Dr. McPhail had reached a different conclusion about the cause of the boy's death based on expert authority and on his personal acquaintance with the child's medical history. Dr. McGill's opinion was her own. Surely, that was "sufficient to cause a doubt." Ludgate concluded by referring to the Depression and the circumstances over which the Bates had no control. It was the first time he had mentioned it during the trial. "The worst that could be said of them," he reflected, "was that they were too proud to accept relief."[41]

Cruise took a different approach. He said that the Crown was sympathetic to the plight of Ted and Rose, that it was a painful case, but he also had a duty to do. "Going on relief was hard on these people," he admitted. "Of course it was, but is that any reason for killing a boy?" For the next three-quarters of an hour, Cruise methodically outlined the journey of the family from Saskatoon to the Avalon schoolyard and how the death of Jackie was part of a sad murder-suicide plot gone terribly wrong. He also attacked the credibility of Dr. McPhail. "What are authorities in the mouth of a man like that?" he asked. "Lots of books could not be compared to the practical experience of Dr. McGill." Above all, he implored the jurors to set aside their feelings. "The crown doesn't want you to convict anybody but to have regard for the facts ... don't be moved by sympathy, compassion or guilt."[42]

Judge MacDonald addressed the jury for about thirty minutes. He started by defining the difference between murder and manslaughter and how manslaughter did not apply in this case—the parents were jointly charged with deliberately bringing about the death of their son. He then suggested that the jury consider three possibilities: that Jackie Bates died at the hands of his parents from carbon monoxide poisoning, that he died accidentally from carbon monoxide poisoning, or that he died from some other cause. If there were any doubt about the reason for the child's death, MacDonald admonished them, then they should not convict. The remainder of the judge's remarks were devoted to a review of the facts of the case as disclosed by the evidence. He sent them off at 5:40 P.M. But before they got down to deciding the fate of the Bates, the jurors took a supper break and did not begin their deliberations until after 7 P.M.

The court, in the meantime, continued with the business on the docket, a separation case between a Biggar couple. That hearing was abruptly interrupted at 9:20 P.M. with the news that the Bates jury was ready with its verdict. Lawyers and witnesses for the separation case stepped aside, while people who had been milling around outside poured back into the courtroom. The tension was palpable.

At 9:35 P.M., Judge MacDonald called on the Bates to stand for the verdict. He then turned to the jury foreman and asked, "How say you?"

"Not guilty," rang out through the hushed room.

The two words brought smiles of relief and even some tears. Ted and Rose embraced in the prisoner's box and then, in the words of a reporter, "stepped out to freedom."[43] Whether they could leave behind the nightmare their lives had become was another matter.

THE HORROR
OF IMAGINING

arry Ludgate's victory in the Wilkie courtroom in March 1934, for which he was paid the grand sum of $150 by the Saskatchewan government, was probably the greatest triumph in his checkered legal career.[1] But did the outcome really belong in the win column for the Saskatoon lawyer? It could reasonably be argued that the prosecution had lost the trial even before the case went to the jury.

Crown prosecutor George Cruise certainly thought so. Two days after the Bates had been acquitted, he reflected on his handling of the case in a revealing letter to the Saskatchewan deputy attorney general. Cruise regretted how Dr. McPhail had attempted to subvert the findings of the provincial pathologist and "may have bluffed the jury somewhat." He also resented any second-guessing over his decision to put the superintendent of the North Battleford Mental Hospital on the stand to discuss Rose's mental fitness. In the end, however, he insisted that the accused had been "proven to be guilty," but that they had been "set free through the sympathy felt by everyone."[2]

Others who had been closely involved in the case had similar reactions. Corporal Carey attributed the acquittal to the capital murder charge. "The jury were satisfied that the accused were legally 'GUILTY,'" he argued in his trial report, "but on account of the severity of the punishment refrained from bringing in a verdict to that effect."[3] One of the jurors told Walter Smyth, Cruise's prosecution partner, the same thing the day after the trial. Patrol Sergeant Williams, on the other hand, believed that the jury was looking for a reason—any reason—to set the Bates free and went for the bait offered by Ludgate. The mere suggestion of thymus death gave the jury "a reasonable doubt upon which to acquit the prisoners."[4] And if it wasn't thymus death, it would have been something else.

The Crown chose not to appeal the verdict, even though it steadfastly stood by the pathologist's report about the cause of Jackie's death. The provincial Department of Justice seemed to appreciate that it had been a difficult trial for all concerned and that a conviction was unlikely if the case were retried.[5]

The decision also went without much comment in the media. Local newspapers seemed more interested in reporting what the Bates planned to do next, now that their four-month ordeal was over.

The couple spent their first night of freedom in Wilkie's Morris Hotel, where the proprietor treated them to a free room. "I want to express our thanks to all our friends and others who have been so good to us," a grateful Ted told a reporter in the hotel lobby. Rose added that they were ready for "a fresh start as soon as possible."[6] Early the next morning, George Couper and another councillor from Glidden called on the pair to take them back by car to the village—probably one of the last places they wanted to go. Before leaving Biggar, Ted announced to the press that he was looking for work, and it was rumoured that they might head north to homestead using the small sum of money that they had been given from a local church fund.

The Bates' whereabouts over the next few years are difficult to determine with any certainty. No mention is made of Glidden in Ted's obituary notice, only that the Bates resided in nearby Eston for a few years before moving to Rosetown in 1939. This was confirmed by Eddie

Morris, who drove to Eston in 1939 to pick up Ted who was going to work as a butcher for the Assily Brothers grocery business in Rosetown.[7]

According to the information they provided on their 1940 National Registration forms, the couple was separated during the first years of the Second World War. Ted was working for the Hellofs butcher business in Kerrobert and did not list his wife as a dependent, while Rose, who identified herself as a homemaker, was—amazingly—back in Glidden and willing to relocate if needed by the war effort. Maybe she had no other place to go and was living in their old house.

The pair did eventually end up together again in Rosetown, where Ted was the butcher in the back of the Red and White grocery store. That's where Harry McDonald, Jackie's childhood friend who was then working as a salesman for General Foods, found him in 1948. Ted insisted on taking Harry home to meet Rose, who broke down on discovering Harry's identity. Throughout dinner, Ted and Rose talked animatedly about their late son and what he had meant to them. McDonald, who had visions of the dead Jackie in his casket, was so unnerved by the experience that he never went back to see them.[8]

Ted Bates died from cancer in Rosetown on 9 December 1954 at the age of sixty-four and was buried in an unmarked grave in the town cemetery. Rose went back to England shortly thereafter to live with her youngest brother, George, in Rotherfield, the same village where she had been born. She died there in Rosemary Cottage almost a quarter century later on 14 February 1978. People there apparently never knew of her Canadian secret.[9]

Long before their passing, though, the dreadful circumstances surrounding Jackie's death were largely forgotten except by those who had some connection to the Bates or the incident. A schoolteacher who arrived in Glidden in 1940 reported that people did not want to talk openly about the tragedy, as if it were something that was best left alone.[10]

William Wardill, a seven-year-old boy in nearby Eatonia at the time of Jackie's death, had a similar experience. While many people knew the Bates and quickly learned the details of their botched suicide attempt, the incident, coming just three weeks before Christmas, was deliberately kept from the children of the village, a surprising feat given the short distance between the two communities. "In an unspoken accord, the older people erected a ring of silence," Wardill related years later in an article. "We were never told about Jack Bates."[11] It was not until he read Pierre Berton's account of the tragedy almost sixty years later that Wardill first became aware of Jackie's fate, even though he regularly travelled to and worked in Glidden in the late 1940s and 1950s and is recognized today as the leading local historian of the area.[12]

Berton was not the first writer to examine the sorry plight of Ted and Rose Bates. In 1983, exactly half a century after eight-year-old Jackie's death, Trent University historian James Struthers attributed the incident to the strict enforcement of municipal residency requirements to reduce relief rolls. "In the eyes of Glidden," Struthers summed up the sad affair in his book *No Fault of Their Own*, "it was the Depression, not the Bates, that had murdered their young son and it was R. B. Bennett's unemployment policy, with its insistence of local responsibility for the jobless, which was a direct accomplice."[13]

Berton expanded upon this theme in his 1990 book *The Great Depression*. In a section subtitled "Death by Depression," he claimed that Ted and Rose were not only tragic victims of mean-spirited relief policies, but also of their own headstrong pride, something that many Canadians struggled to overcome at the time.[14] That's why the Bates were found not guilty at their trial—a verdict that was applauded, according to Berton, because people understood the dilemma faced by the family.

Today, the Bates story is often cited as one of the more harrowing episodes of the so-called decade of despair. A Canadian university-level textbook, for example, uses the tragedy to open the chapter on the Great Depression.[15] In fact, Ted and Rose have come to epitomize the collateral damage wrought by the collapse of rural Saskatchewan in the early 1930s.[16] But were the hard times, Canada's relief policies, and parents' pride directly to blame for what happened that cold night in the Avalon schoolyard in December 1933? Or were they simply extenuating circumstances?

Those who knew Ted and Rose Bates readily accepted their explanation for their actions without question. The alternative—that the pair had planned to murder their son in cold blood—was unthinkable. The strange thing, however, is that Harry Ludgate never did put the Depression on trial in Wilkie. Maybe he believed it was an unspoken subtext to the proceedings. Clearly, the prosecution witnesses were doing a good job of demonstrating how the "Dirty Thirties" had effectively destroyed the lives of the Bates family. Or maybe he realized that Jackie's death had more to do with the couple's troubled existence than people who knew Ted and Rose were willing to admit. Whatever the reason, Ludgate never made the Depression the centrepiece of his defence of the Bates. Instead, he concentrated on *how* Jackie died by challenging the validity of the pathologist's report.

The *why* was another matter. For the Bates, the Depression was a ready-made alibi for taking their son's life, even though personal problems were at the root of the tragedy—personal problems that had brought Ted and Rose to the precipice of something catastrophic well before the family set off from Saskatoon in the rental car that cold December morning. In fact, according to closed records secured through access to information requests, Rose had threatened to take her life and that of Jackie before the twin scourge of depression and drought had staggered Glidden. She might even have been suicidal before she immigrated to Canada.

The sad truth, as revealed in internal RCMP reports and the provincial Department of Justice case file, was that Ted and Rose were unhappy partners in a bitter marriage held together by their struggle over their only child. Giving up Jackie, one of the last things they had in the world when the Depression had taken everything else, was impossible for either of them. In their selfishness, they decided to kill him and themselves when they had lost all hope.

In one of the most poignant passages about Jackie's murder at the hands of his parents, William Wardill thanked the people of Eatonia for keeping the boy's death a secret. "The cordon of silence imposed by our elders," he wrote in 2000, "saved us from the horror of imagining that, while we read our books, people we loved and trusted might kill us with a stealthy, lethal gas."[17]

Jackie Bates was thankfully spared that horror, only because he died in his sleep from carbon monoxide poisoning, lying between the two people he most loved and trusted in the world.

Note on Approach and Sources

Who Killed Jackie Bates? seeks to recreate the troubled lives and desperate times of Ted and Rose Bates and explain what drove them, as part of a double suicide, to murder their only child in an isolated schoolyard in rural Saskatchewan on a cold December night in 1933. The story is deliberately written with an immediacy that goes beyond a more traditional narrative approach in order to provide a better understanding and appreciation of the circumstances behind the sorry incident. Any recreations are scrupulously based on a careful and close reading of the sources, as are the few instances of speculation or conjecture. The words spoken throughout the book are also taken verbatim from the sources and serve to reinforce that the Bates were not simply helpless victims of the Depression, but flawed people with complex personalities. The background material, meanwhile, is intended to provide insight into a time and place that seems light years away from the Canada of today.

The major sources for the book were secured through access to information requests. The Bates murder file, stamped closed two months after the March 1934 trial, was still held at Royal Canadian Mounted Police Headquarters in Ottawa. Similarly, the provincial Department of Justice file on the case had never been transferred to the Saskatchewan Archives Board and was located and made available to the author in response to a formal request. These documents, which included copies of personal correspondence, suggested that Jackie's death was much more than a Depression tragedy. Other materials included court documents (coroner's inquest and preliminary hearing) found in the basement of the old Battleford courthouse. The author also conducted a number of interviews with people who had some connection to the incident and/or who had known some of the individuals involved. Finally, extensive use was made of local histories and Saskatchewan newspapers to flesh out the story and provide context and perspective.

The endnotes are largely limited to direct quotes and interviews.

ACKNOWLEDGEMENTS

Who Killed Jackie Bates? greatly benefitted from the generous assistance of many people. The research, writing, and production of the book would not have been such a rewarding experience without their kind help. People were fascinated by the incident and were just as interested in coming to a better understanding of the story as I was.

Nadine Charabin, Sherri Fowler, Janet Harvey, Patrick Hayes, Steve Hewitt, David Horky, Tim Novak, Myrna Petersen, Linda Putz, Michelle Schmidt, Lenora Toth, and Glenn Wright helped identify and secure archival materials. Jacki Andre, Selena Crosson, and Peter Norman provided invaluable research assistance. Merle Massie, in keeping with her character, was especially diligent in this regard and turned up a number of promising leads. Jean Barman, Bill Barry, John Belshaw, Chris Kent, Dave Lepard, Robert McDonald, Betty McManus, Danny Pagé, Darlene Ruckle, and Jean Taylor supplied information on the Glidden/Madison and Biggar/Purdue districts, 1930s Vancouver or late-nineteenth-century London. Cliff Moore took me on a personal tour of the Prince Albert penitentiary. Steve Angel and Gary Wobeser ably commented on Jackie's autopsy. Lu-Anne Demetrick, Dave McLay, and a number of other individuals identified in the endnotes talked about the key personalities in the story—either by e-mail, over the telephone, or in their homes and offices. Brendan Kelly handled a number of tasks associated with the research and writing of the book with his usual efficiency.

Harry McDonald and William Wardill, two fine gentlemen who grew up in Glidden and Eatonia, respectively, faithfully read the draft chapters as they were written and provided helpful and encouraging feedback along the way. It was a treat to work with them. Bill Brennan, Gerry Hallowell, Stuart Houston, Jim Miller, Peter MacKinnon, and Garrett Wilson found time in their busy schedules to provide expert commentary on the draft manuscript, especially on the legal and medical aspects. Their advice made it a better book, for which I am extremely grateful. Naturally, any errors are my own doing.

Brian Smith and Mike McCoy of Articulate Eye Design of Saskatoon prepared the maps and digitally enhanced the newspaper photographs.

Marilyn St. Marie of St. Solo Graphics did scans of several of the photographs. Dean Pickup nicely captured the essence of the story with his design.

Then, there are the women who make Fifth House the finest publisher of non-fiction on the prairies: Lesley Reynolds who skillfully edited the story with care and sensitivity; Meaghan Craven who ensured that the manuscript sailed safely through production as if it were her own work; Lyn Cadence who was forever thinking of ways to promote the story; and Charlene Dobmeier who has a keen sense of what makes a good book and applies these same standards to the press itself. *Who Killed Jackie Bates?* marks a wonderfully rewarding twenty-year relationship with Fifth House.

Finally, my family—especially Marley—has always been supportive, always interested and enthusiastic, about my latest book project. It's made a real difference to my life, let alone my writing.

NOTES

INTRODUCTION: WE HAVE BEEN MIXING THINGS UP

1. Saskatchewan Justice [hereafter SJ], *R. v. Bates*, "Edward Alfred Bates–Murder" memorandum, 9 December 1933.

2. Ibid., "Coroner's Inquest touching the death of Jack Edward Bates," Biggar, 14–15 December 1933.

3. Ibid.

4. Ibid.

5. Ibid.

CHAPTER ONE: EVERYONE LIKED HIM

1. The author has been unable to locate Ted Bates on any of the ships sailing from Great Britain during these years. His 1914 information is taken from the S.S. *Victorian* manifest.

2. This information was secured from census data for 1891 and 1901. Genealogist Peter Norman kindly conducted the search in British records.

3. Quoted in W. A. Waiser, *The Field Naturalist: John Macoun, Natural Science, and the Geological Survey* (Toronto: University of Toronto Press, 1989), 53.

4. W. C. Pollard, *Pioneering in the Prairie West* (London: A.H. Stockwell, n.d.), 49 [emphasis added].

5. Starting in 1940, under the authority of the National Resources Mobilization Act, all persons sixteen years or older were required to complete a questionnaire to facilitate the mobilization of Canada's human resources for the war effort. The form required the registrant to provide detailed information on a number of matters, including place and country of birth (and parents), occupation, previous military service, and date of entry into Canada (if an immigrant). The National Registration forms, arranged by electoral district, can be accessed today through Statistics Canada. Unfortunately, Ted Bates did not indicate on his form what year he first arrived in Canada.

6. The personal information about Rose Bates is based on census material and on her 1940 National Registration form.

7. Between 1921 and 1924, the Department of Immigration and Colonization required all individuals arriving at Canadian ports of entry to complete a separate form or individual manifest (Form 30A). The documents were microfilmed in quasi-alphabetical order (groupings based on the initial letters of surnames).

8. The CN passenger and mixed trains ran from Saskatoon southwest to Delisle, then south to Conquest and Tichfield, then northeast to Surbiton before continuing west to Glidden. See *Waghorn's Guide* for the exact route and times.

9. Harry McDonald to Bill Waiser, personal communication, 4 September 2002.

10. *Saskatoon Star-Phoenix*, 7 December 1933.

11. Saskatchewan Justice [hereafter SJ], *R. v. Bates*, Rose Bates to Helena Butler, n.d. The date is sometime in 1932, since Rose says twice in the letter that she has been married to Ted for eight years.

12. McDonald to Waiser, 4 September 2002; William Wardill interview, 23 November 2005.

13. Neil Reimer interview, 9 November 2005.

14. Library and Archives Canada, Manuscript Division, R. B. Bennett papers, 489488, G. V. Couper to R. B. Bennett, 18 December 1933.

15. Gladys Arthur interview, 31 October 2005; Pete Abelseth interview, 9 November 2005; Marie Urlacker interview, 23 November 2005; Jean Hart interview, 12 December 2005; Phyllis Nemrova interview, 12 December 2005.

16. *As It Happened: A History of the R.M. of Newcombe #260* (Madison, Sask.: RM of Newcombe History Committee, 1992), 52, 55.

17. SJ, *R. v. Bates*, W. O. Smyth to Deputy Attorney General, 20 December 1933.

18. Eunice Seekins interview, 12 December 2005.

CHAPTER TWO: JUST ABOUT OUT OF MY MIND

1. Harry McDonald interview, 9–10 December 2005.

2. In September 1934, D. B. Macrae and R.M. Scott toured the so-called "burnt out" area of southern Saskatchewan and filed stories along the way. D. B. Macrae and R. M. Scott, *In the South Country* (Saskatoon: Star-Phoenix, 1934), 13.

3. Sinclair Ross, *As for Me and My House* (Toronto: McClelland and Stewart, 1957), 96.

4. Edna Jacques, *Drifting Soil* (Moose Jaw: Moose Jaw Times Co. Ltd., n.d.), 12.

5. T. M. Healey, "Engendering Resistance: Women Respond to Relief in Saskatoon, 1930–1932," in *"Other" Voices: Historical Essays on Saskatchewan Women*, eds. D. De Brou and A. Moffatt (Regina: Canadian Plains Research Centre, 1995), 94–115.

6. M. Hobbs, "Equality and Difference: Feminism and the Defence of Women Workers During the Great Depression," *Labour/Le Travail* 32 (fall 1993): 215.

7. Quoted in L. M. Grayson and M. Bliss, eds., *The Wretched of Canada: Letters to R. B. Bennett, 1930–1935* (Toronto: McClelland and Stewart, 1971), 112.

8. Quoted in A. Lawton, "Urban Relief in Saskatchewan During the Years of the Depression, 1930–39" (M.A. thesis, University of Saskatchewan, 1969), 37.

9. Quoted in Grayson and Bliss, eds., *The Wretched of Canada*, 54. Although the letter-writer identified her Saskatchewan community as Kingdom, the place name is not on any provincial map. Nor was the author able to find Lambert (n. 11) or Harney (n. 12).

10. Ibid., 147.

11. Ibid., 76.

12. Ibid., 38.

13. Library and Archives Canada, Manuscript Division, R. B. Bennett papers, 489416, W. C. Murray to R. B. Bennett, 5 September 1933.

14. M. Braithwaite, *Why Shoot the Teacher* (Toronto: McClelland and Stewart, 1967), 5.

15. Phyllis Nemrova interview, 12 December 2005.

16. Saskatchewan Justice [hereafter SJ], *R. v. Bates*, Rose Bates to Helena Butler, n.d.

17. *Vancouver Sun*, 8 December 1933.

18. J. D. Belshaw, "The Administration of Relief to the Unemployed in Vancouver during the Great Depression" (M.A. thesis, University of British Columbia, 1979), 28, 37, 98, 126. The author wishes to thank Belshaw for kindly providing a copy of his thesis.

19. Quoted in *Vancouver Sun*, 8 December 1933.

20. *Saskatoon Star-Phoenix*, 15 December 1933.

21. Quoted in *Vancouver Sun*, 9 September 1933.

22. SJ, "Statement of C. H. Babcock of 1016 Main St., Vancouver, B.C.," 9 January 1934.

23. Quoted in *Saskatoon Star-Phoenix*, 20 March 1934.

24. Quoted in *Vancouver Sun*, 9 September 1933.

25. Quoted in *Saskatoon Star-Phoenix*, 20 March 1934.

CHAPTER THREE: THEY WON'T HAVE US HERE

1. E. B. Mitchell, *In Western Canada Before the War* (London: J. Murray, 1915), 74.

2. Quoted in S. D. Hanson, ed., *A Prairie Memoir: The Life and Times of James Clinkskill, 1853–1936* (Regina: Canadian Plains Research Center, 2003), 150.

3. Saskatchewan Justice [hereafter SJ], *R. v. Bates*, "Edward Alfred Bates–Murder" memorandum, 14 December 1933.

4. *Saskatoon Star-Phoenix*, 20 March 1934.

5. SJ, "Coroner's Inquest touching the death of Jack Edward Bates," Biggar, 14–15 December 1933.

6. Quoted in *Globe and Mail*, 27 June 1998.

7. P. Berton, *The Great Depression, 1929–1939* (Toronto: McClelland and Stewart, 1990), 188.

8. SJ, *R. v. Bates*, T. Bates to C. H. Babcock, 2 December 1933.

9. Quoted in *Vancouver Sun*, 8 December 1933.

10. SJ, *R. v. Bates*, T. Bates to S. Elliot, 2 December 1933.

11. Ibid., "Edward Alfred Bates–Murder" memorandum, 29 December 1933.

12. Ibid., R. Bates to Mr. and Mrs. F. Gardiner, n.d.

13. Ibid., "Edward Alfred Bates–Murder" memorandum, 29 December 1933.

14. Big Little Books (measuring 3 ½ inches by 4 ½ inches and about 1 ½ inches thick) were extremely popular at the time. The text was on the left-hand side of each page, a black and white illustration on the right. Sometimes children coloured the illustrations. Jackie's books were 731 and 734 in the series.

15. SJ, *R. v. Bates*, "Edward Alfred Bates–Murder" memorandum, 18 December 1933.

16. Ibid.

CHAPTER FOUR: LET'S GO IN HERE AND FINISH IT

1. Keppel Block #1 was established along the border shared by the Perdue (No. 346) and Biggar (No. 347) rural municipalities, while the other two blocks were to the west (Keppel #2) and east (Keppel #3) of Cando. All three sections were transferred to the province in 1931. Keppel #1 became part of the Perdue Grazing Co-operative. This information was kindly supplied by Bill Barry.

2. The Hanson buck, with a world record Boone and Crockett score of 213 5/8, was shot in the region on 23 November 1993.

3. Frank Weekes interview, 10 November 2005.

4. Saskatchewan Justice [hereafter SJ], "Coroner's Inquest touching the death of Jack Edward Bates," Biggar, 14–15 December 1933.

5. Ibid.

6. SJ, *R. v. Bates*, D. McLay, "Murder of John Bates, Biggar District, Saskatchewan," 7 December 1933.

7. SJ, "Coroner's Inquest touching the death of Jack Edward Bates," Biggar, 14–15 December 1933.

8. Reproduced in McLay, "Murder of John Bates, Biggar District, Saskatchewan," 7 December 1933.

9. Ibid.

10. Ibid.

11. Ibid.

12. Ibid.

13. Ibid.

14. Ibid.

15. Ibid.

CHAPTER FIVE: I KNOW WE'LL HANG

1. Royal Canadian Mounted Police [hereafter RCMP], Edward and Rose Bates murder file, C. E. Carey, "Report on Preliminary Hearing," 8 December 1933.

2. Ibid., D. McLay memorandum, 7 December 1933.

3. Anne (Evanoff) Worobey interview, 23 January 2005.

4. RCMP, Carey, "Report on Preliminary Hearing," 8 December 1933.

5. Quoted in Saskatchewan Justice [hereafter SJ], *R. v. Bates*, C. E. Carey memorandum, 20 December 1933.

6. Quoted in RCMP, Bates murder file, C. E. Carey, "Report on Preliminary Hearing," 21 December 1933.

7. Reproduced in SJ, *R. v. Bates*, McLay memorandum, 7 December 1933.

8. Quoted in RCMP, Bates murder file, C. E. Carey, "Report on Preliminary Hearing," 21 December 1933.

9. Ibid.

10. Quoted in Ibid., "Edward Alfred Bates, Murder (263) C.C.C.," 7 December 1933.

11. Ibid., H. W. H. Williams memorandum, 7 December 1933.

12. SJ, W. O. Smyth to Deputy Attorney General, 20 December 1933.

13. Ibid., C. E. Carey memorandum, 21 December 1933.

14. *Vancouver Sun*, 9 December 1933.

15. *Edmonton Journal*, 8 December 1933.

16. Library and Archives Canada [hereafter LAC], Manuscript Division, R. B. Bennett papers, 489488, G. V. Couper to R. B. Bennett, 18 December 1933.

17. Harry McDonald interview, 9–10 December 2005.

18. RCMP, Carey Memorandum, 21 December 1933.

19. The author wishes to thank Drs. Steve Angel and Gary Wobeser for their kind help with the autopsy report.

20. Lila Sully interview, 22 August 2007.

21. Ibid., Williams memorandum, 7 December 1933.

22. LAC, Bennett papers, 489460-1, Couper to Bennett, 9 December 1933.

23. Western Development Museum, G. V. Couper to Station Agent, Clair, Saskatchewan, 20 January 1934.

24. Betty (Reimer) Sawatzky interview, 31 October 2005; Neil Reimer interview, 9 November 2005.

25. McDonald interview, 9–10 December 2005.

26. Jean (Stannard) Hart interview, 12 December 2005.

CHAPTER SIX: CERTAINLY LOVED BY BOTH

1. *Saskatoon Star-Phoenix*, 12 December 1933.

2. Ibid., 7 December 1933.

3. *Saskatchewan Justice* [hereafter SJ], *R. v. Bates*, H. W. H. Williams, "Biggar Detachment Case" memorandum, 9 December 1933.

4. Quoted in Royal Canadian Mounted Police [hereafter RCMP], Edward and Rose Bates murder file, C. E. Carey, "Rose (Mrs. Edward Alfred) BATES Murder (263) C.C.C. of John Bates, Biggar District, Saskatchewan," 11 December 1933.

5. Quoted in SJ, *R. v. Bates*, W. Lambert, "Edward BATES Murder, Perdue, Saskatchewan," 12 December 1933.

6. *Saskatoon Star-Phoenix*, 11 December 1933.

7. Quoted in SJ, *R. v. Bates*, Statement of Mrs. Kemp, Night Matron, 21 December 1933.

8. Much of the material on Walter Smyth's background and character was kindly provided by his daughter Lu-Anne Demetrick in an e-mail dated 4 January 2006.

9. T. Gauley interview, 3 October 2005; D. S. McKercher interview, 17 October 2005; R. Carter interview, 2 December 2005; C. F. Tallis interview, 2 January 2006.

10. H. W. McConnell, *Prairie Justice* (Calgary, 1980), 78.

11. The inquest testimony has been quoted from SJ, "Coroner's Inquest touching the death of Jack Bates," transcript, 14 December 1933.

12. Gauley interview, 3 October 2005.

13. The quotations from the preliminary hearing can be found in SJ, "Rex vs. Rose Bates and Edward A. Bates," transcript, 15 December 1933.

14. *Saskatoon Star-Phoenix*, 15 December 1933.

CHAPTER SEVEN: BETTER LUCK THAN US

1. *Criminal Code of Canada* (Ottawa: King's Printer, 1927), 85–6.

2. Library and Archives Canada [hereafter LAC], Manuscript Division, R. B. Bennett papers, 489489, G. V. Couper to R. B. Bennett, 18 December 1933.

3. Saskatchewan Justice [hereafter SJ], *R. v. Bates*, C. E. Carey, "Report on Preliminary Hearing," memorandum, 18 December 1933 [emphasis added].

4. Ibid.

5. Ibid., R. Bates to Mr. and Mrs. F. Gardiner, n.d.

6. Ibid., Rose Bates to Helena Butler, n.d.

7. Ibid., W. O. Smyth to Deputy Attorney General, 18 December 1933.

8. LAC, Bennett Papers, 489488, Couper to Bennett, 18 December 1933.

9. Cliff Moore, chief of education at the Saskatchewan Penitentiary in Prince Albert, kindly provided information on the Prince Albert jail, as well as arranged a tour of the federal prison.

10. SJ, *R. v. Bates*, J. W. MacNeill to A. Blackwood, 6 January 1934.

11. Janet Harvey of the Saskatchewan Archives Board kindly helped secure access to these records.

12. Quoted in S. Skinner et al., *Corrections: An Historical Perspective of the Saskatchewan Experience* (Regina: Canadian Plains Research Center, 1981), 61.

13. Ibid., 44.

14. SJ, *R. v. Bates*, W. Lambert memorandum, 27 December 1933.

15. Ibid., J. R. O'Reilly memorandum, 11 January 1934.

16. Ibid.

17. Ibid., T. Bates to C. H. Babcock, 2 December 1933.

18. Ibid., J. R. O'Reilly memorandum, 11 January 1934.

19. Quoted in ibid.

20. Ibid.

21. Royal Canadian Mounted Police [hereafter RCMP], Edward and Rose Bates murder file, J. H. MacBrien to H. Guthrie, 28 December 1933.

22. See G. Wilson and K. Wilson, *Diefenbaker for the Defence* (Toronto: James Lorimerk, 1988), chapter 10.

23. "Rex v. Bohun," *Western Weekly Reports* 3 (1933): 612.

24. Ibid., 610.

25. Quoted in SJ, *R. v. Bates*, E. J. Des Rosiers memorandum, 23 January 1934.

26. Quoted in ibid., C. E. Carey memorandum, 18 January 1934.

27. Ibid., A.L. Seaman memorandum, 26 January 1934.

28. Ibid., G. A. Cruise to A. Blackwood, 5 February 1934.

29. Ibid., G. A. Cruise to A. Blackwood, 14 February 1934.

30. Ibid., G. A. Cruise to W. O. Smyth, 7 February 1934.

31. Ibid., G. A. Cruise to A. Blackwood, 14 February 1934.

32. Ibid., W. O. Smyth to G. A Cruise, 24 February 1934.

CHAPTER EIGHT: THE FIGHT FOR THEIR LIVES

1. Frank Anderson provides a case-by-case history of women condemned to death in Canada in *A Dance with Death: Canadian Women on the Gallows, 1754–1954* (Saskatoon: Fifth House Publishers, 1996).

2. The Lassandro story was the subject of the opera, "Filumena," which premiered in Calgary in 2003, seventy years after her execution.

3. Saskatchewan Justice [hereafter SJ], *R. v. Bates*, G. A. Cruise to A. Blackwood, 17 February 1934.

4. Western Development Museum, G. V. Couper to Station Agent, Clair, Saskatchewan, 20 January 1934.

5. Ibid.

6. SJ, *R. v. Bates*, H. Ludgate to Minister of Municipal Affairs, 6 March 1934.

7. Ibid., G. A. Cruise to W. O. Smyth, 7 December 1934.

8. Ibid.

9. Ibid.

10. *Edmonton Journal*, 22 March 1934.

11. Royal Canadian Mounted Police [hereafter RCMP], Edward and Rose Bates murder file, H. W. H. Williams, "Biggar District case," 24 March 1934.

12. SJ, G. A. Cruise to A. Blackwood, 24 March 1934.

13. Some of the jurors were found in the Wilkie community history book, *A Harvest of Memories: A History of Rural Wilkie*, 2 vols. (Wilkie, Sask.: Eighty Year History Society, 1984).

14. Quoted in *Saskatoon Star-Phoenix*, 20 March 1934.

15. William Bahrey was hanged for murder in the Prince Albert jail on 23 February 1934.

16. Quoted in *Saskatoon Star-Phoenix*, 21 March 1934.

17. Ibid.

18. Ibid.

19. Ibid.

20. Ibid.

21. Ibid.

22. SJ, *R. v. Bates*, G. A. Cruise to W. O. Smyth, 7 February 1934.

23. Quoted in *Saskatoon Star-Phoenix*, 22 March 1934.

24. Ibid.

25. Ibid.

26. For an historical account of the disease, see Ann Dally, "Status Lymphaticus: Sudden Death in Children from 'Visitation of God' to Cot Death," *Medical History* 47 (1997): 70–85. Gary Wobeser kindly provided a copy of this article to the author.

27. SJ, *R. v. Bates,*, G. A. Cruise to A. Blackwood, 24 March 1934.

28. Ibid.

29. Quoted in *Saskatoon Star-Phoenix*, 22 March 1934.

30. Ibid.

31. Biographical material on McPhail was generously provided by Dr. Stuart Houston.

32. W. Wardill interview, 23 November 2005.

33. SJ, *R. v. Bates*, "Affidavit of Harry Ludgate," 15 March 1934.

34. Quoted in *Saskatoon Star-Phoenix*, 22 March 1934.

35. Ibid.

36. *Saskatoon Star-Phoenix*, 22 March 1934; *Regina Leader-Post*, 22 March 1934.

37. Quoted in *Saskatoon Star-Phoenix*, 23 March 1934.

38. Ibid.

39. Ibid.

40. Ibid.

41. Ibid.

42. Ibid.

43. Ibid.

EPILOGUE: THE HORROR OF IMAGINING

1. The prosecution team of Cruise and Smyth billed the Saskatchewan government $580 ($314 and $266, respectively).

2. Saskatchewan Justice [hereafter SJ] SJ *R. v. Bates*, G. A. Cruise to A. Blackwood, 24 March 1934.

3. Royal Canadian Mounted Police [hereafter RCMP], "Edward Alfred Bates et al murder, C. E. Carey, Report on Conclusion of Case," 24 March 1934.

4. Ibid., H. W. H. Williams, "Biggar Detachment Case," 24 March 1934.

5. Since the case never went to appeal, no official transcript of the trial was kept.

6. Quoted in *Saskatoon Star-Phoenix*, 23 March 1934.

7. Eddie Morris interview, 31 October 2005.

8. Harry McDonald interview, 9–10 December 2005.

9. Don Coe, e-mail communication to Bill Waiser, 20 August 2007.

10. Bessie Hammel interview, 30 November 2005.

11. W. Wardill, "The Frog Lake Burials and other stories," *The Spear Grass Scripts*, folio 3 (2000), 11.

12. W. Wardill interview, 23 November 2005.

13. James Struthers, *No Fault of Their Own: Unemployment and the Canadian Welfare State, 1914–1941* (Toronto: University of Toronto Press, 1983), 84.

14. P. Berton, *The Great Depression, 1929–1939* (Toronto: McClelland and Stewart, 1990), 188.

15. M. Conrad and A. Finkel, *History of the Canadian Peoples, v. 2, 1867 to present* (Toronto: Pearson Longman, 2006), 231.

16. A summary of the Pierre Berton account of the tragedy appears in the Glidden community history book amidst the other family stories. It has become the standard account of the Bates incident and part of the local memory. See *As It Happened: History of the R.M. of Newcombe #260* (Madison, Sask.: RM of Newcombe History Committee, 1992), 204.

17. Wardill, "The Frog Lake Burials and other stories," 12.

ABOUT BILL WAISER

Photo by Sean Francis Martin

A specialist in western and northern Canadian history, Bill Waiser joined the Department of History at the University of Saskatchewan in 1984 and served as department head from 1995–98. He was Yukon Historian for the Canadian Parks Service prior to his university appointment.

Bill has published eleven books, including *Park Prisoners: The Untold Story of Western Canada's National Parks* and (with Blair Stonechild) *Loyal till Death: Indians and the North-West Rebellion*, which was a finalist for the 1997 Governor General's literary award for non-fiction. His *All Hell Can't Stop Us: The On-to-Ottawa Trek and Regina Riot* won the 2003 Saskatchewan Book Award for non-fiction. He is perhaps best known for his centennial history of the province, *Saskatchewan: A New History*.

Bill was named the university's Distinguished Researcher at the spring 2004 convocation and received the College of Arts and Science Teaching Excellence Award in 2003. He was awarded the Saskatchewan Order of Merit, the province's highest honour, in 2006, and was elected a fellow of the Royal Society of Canada the following year.

Bill is a recreational runner who also likes to garden, hike, and canoe.